Vegetar

FOOD for FRIENDS

THE VEGETARIAN SOCIETY'S

Vegetarian
FOOD for FRIENDS

Lyn **Weller**

Foreword by Breakfast TV's Fiona Phillips

HarperCollins*Publishers*

First published in 1998 by HarperCollins*Publishers*

This paperback edition published in 2000 by
HarperCollins*Illustrated*

www.**fire**and**water**.com
The book lovers website

Text © The Vegetarian Society UK Ltd 1998
Photographs © HarperCollins*Publishers* 1998

The Vegetarian Society asserts the moral right
to be identified as the author of this work.

A catalogue record for this book is available from the British Library.

ISBN 0 00 414109 1

Designed and produced by SP Creative Design
Editor: Heather Thomas
Design and production: Rolando Ugolini

Photography: Chris Alack

Colour origination by Colourscan, Singapore
Printed and bound by Rotolito Lombarda SpA, Milan, Italy

Acknowledgement

Lyn Weller would like to extend her warmest thanks to all the people who have
helped in producing this book. In particular to Barbara Dixon of HarperCollins and
Heather Thomas for guiding me through the process and arranging the layout and
photography. Also to Tina Fox, Chief Executive of The Vegetarian Society, for giving
me the opportunity to write this book. I would particularly like to thank the staff of
the Cordon Vert Cookery School – Vanessa Thrift and Gayle Brister – for their
support and for helping to test the recipes, and all the staff from The Vegetarian
Society who acted as tasters and cleared their plates with such enthusiasm! Thanks
also to Jem Gardener of Vinceremos Wines and Spirits Ltd, Leeds, for providing an
interesting selection of vegetarian and vegan wines for many of the recipes. Finally, a
special thanks to Phil Pugh, my partner, for his support throughout the project.

Vegetarian and vegan wines are available by mail order from:
Vinceremos Wines and Spirits Ltd
261 Upper Town Street
Leeds LS13 3JT
Tel: 0113 257 7545
Fax: 0113 257 6906

The Vegetarian Society exists to promote, and
provide information on, a vegetarian diet for
the benefit of animal welfare, human health
and the environment. Established in 1847, the
Society is the acknowledged expert on
vegetarianism and all aspects relating to the
diet, and produces information sheets, leaflets,
videos and other material.

The Society runs its own cookery school,
Cordon Vert, which provides day, weekend and
week courses ranging from their Diploma
course and professional tuition to leisure
courses for the beginner or the more
adventurous cook wanting to expand their
repertoire.

The Society also works with major food
manufacturers and retailers to improve the
quality, quantity and variety of vegetarian food
available, and administers its own licence
scheme for approved products.

Lyn Weller is manager of The Vegetarian Society's
world-renowned Cordon Vert Cookery School.
Lyn has years of experience with vegetarian cuisine,
having previously run her own vegetarian catering
business and tutored at the cookery school. Her
passion for delicious, healthy food and her
commitment to vegetarianism had earlier led her to
a complete career change from life as a chartered
accountant to pursue her love of vegetarian food.
Lyn believes there are no limits to how varied and
exciting vegetarian food can be, for her, a passion
for food is an appetite for life itself. Lyn lives in
Cheshire near the headquarters of The Vegetarian
Society and spends her spare time gardening,
walking and developing new recipes.

CONTENTS

FOREWORD
BY FIONA PHILLIPS

Many's the time a dinner party invitation has thrown me into a state of panic. It's not that I don't want to go; it's the thought of returning the kind favour that fills me with dread, because 'food for friends' is a difficult concept when you're vegetarian and the majority of your eating companions are not. If you recognise that dilemma, then this book is for you, and for those friends who believe that a meat-less meal is a treat-less meal.

My closest friend, my husband, was a meat-eater and a conscientious tofu objector. So, on a mission to moderate his eating habits, I've bombarded him with the end results of the recipes on the following pages. The progress report so far is... it's working!

Food for Friends is, in part, divided into seasonal sections, so whether food for your friends means converting your partner, a lazy afternoon dining *al fresco*, or a warming winter feast by a roaring fire, there's a recipe to match — and details on great drinks too, to make it all go with a punch!

Cooking for friends is an enjoyable, sociable and yet very personal experience and, when you're vegetarian, the food you serve up speaks for your values too. I know you'll treasure this book and, believe me, the more you use *Food for Friends*, the more friends you'll have.

INTRODUCTION
BY LYN WELLER
COOKERY SCHOOL MANAGER, THE VEGETARIAN SOCIETY

Sharing good food and being creative in the kitchen is what *Vegetarian Food for Friends* is all about. This collection of recipes has dishes suitable for all occasions, from formal dinner parties to *al fresco* summer eating.

The recipes have been devised by the Vegetarian Society's very own Cordon Vert Cookery School. The collection reflects the exciting international range of cookery styles taught on the Cordon Vert courses, including imaginative dishes from Malaysia, Thailand, Italy, France and the Mediterranean. Useful hints and tips for both the beginner and the more experienced cook are given throughout the book.

In some chapters full menus have been suggested, but recipes can be mixed and matched depending on the occasion. Many of the dishes are suitable for vegans or can be adapted easily for vegans.

The Cordon Vert Cookery School encourages anyone interested in cooking, from amateur to professional, to explore the exciting colours and flavours of global vegetarian cuisine and to share the pleasure with friends, old and new. This collection reveals just how tantalising vegetarian food can be. Enjoy.

INFORMAL
SUPPERS

*Left: Exotic vegetable stir-fry (page 22) and Halloumi
and mango with a mint dressing (page 10)*

HALLOUMI AND MANGO
WITH A MINT DRESSING

H alloumi and mango are a really delicious combination. Cook the Halloumi just before serving; if allowed to go cold, it quickly becomes rubbery in texture.

250 g/9 oz Halloumi cheese
6 tablespoons seasoned flour
200 g/7 oz mixed salad leaves
1 ripe mango, peeled, stoned
  and sliced
8 g/$^1/_3$ oz mint, finely chopped

150 ml/5 fl oz natural yogurt
juice of $^1/_2$ lemon
salt and freshly ground black pepper
3 tablespoons groundnut oil
100 g/4 oz cherry tomatoes, halved
sprigs of mint, to garnish

■ Cut the Halloumi into 8 slices and then cut each in half. Coat in the seasoned flour and put aside. Arrange the salad leaves on 4 serving plates and place the slices of mango on top.
■ Make the dressing: mix the chopped mint, yogurt and lemon juice together in a bowl and season to taste.
■ Heat the oil in a non-stick frying pan or griddle and quickly fry the Halloumi for about 2 minutes on each side, until golden.
■ Drizzle the yogurt dressing over the salad leaves and mango. Arrange the fried Halloumi on top. Garnish with cherry tomatoes and mint sprigs and serve immediately with extra dressing on the side.

Serves 4 as a starter or 2 as a main course

Hot and Sour
SOUP

Chinese hot and sour soup usually involves shredded meat, but can easily be made vegetarian by using marinated tofu in its place. Adjust the shoyu, chilli and sesame oil to suit your own taste.

4 dried shiitake mushrooms
1.2 litres/2 pints vegetable stock
225 g/8 oz canned bamboo shoots, drained and shredded
225 g/8 oz marinated tofu, cut into thin strips
2 small red chillies, deseeded and finely chopped
3 tablespoons white wine vinegar
2 tablespoons shoyu
1 tablespoon cornflour
4 tablespoons water
1 free-range egg, beaten (omit for vegans*)
2 teaspoons toasted sesame oil
2 spring onions, shredded

TIP
■

You can use fresh shiitake mushrooms in this soup if you prefer. Wipe the caps and remove and discard the stems before slicing and continue as before. Dried shiitake mushrooms can be purchased very cheaply in Chinese supermarkets where they are usually labelled as 'Dried Mushrooms'.

■ Soak the dried mushrooms in hot water for about 15–20 minutes. Drain through fine muslin, reserving the liquid. Remove the stalks from the mushrooms and discard. Slice the mushrooms into thin strips.
■ Place the mushrooms in a saucepan with the stock and bring to the boil. Simmer for 10 minutes. Add the bamboo shoots, marinated tofu and chillies and simmer for a further 5 minutes. Add the vinegar and shoyu.
■ Mix the cornflour with the water until a paste is formed and add to the soup, stirring all the time until thickened.
■ Take the soup off the heat and stir in the beaten egg, if using. Season with the toasted sesame oil and garnish with spring onion shreds.

Serves 4

SOUPE
AU PISTOU

A hearty, warming peasant soup — good to come home to after a wintry walk with friends or weekend guests. It can be prepared in advance and reheated when required.

TIP

■

In the summer when basil is plentiful and can be grown in your garden, make your own pesto. Put a handful of basil into a blender jug with one or two cloves of crushed garlic, 25 g/1 oz pine kernels, a pinch of salt, 1 tablespoon lemon juice and 4–6 tablespoons of olive oil. Blend well.

4 tablespoons olive oil
1 large onion, finely chopped
2 garlic cloves, crushed
2 sticks celery, finely chopped
225 g/8 oz carrots, finely diced
2 x 425-g/15-oz cans cannellini
   beans, drained and rinsed
900 ml/1½ pints vegetable stock
425-g/15-oz can chopped tomatoes

2 tablespoons tomato purée
3 tablespoons vegan pesto
salt and freshly ground black pepper

To serve:
50 g/2 oz vegetarian Parmesan
cheese, grated (omit for vegans)
crusty French bread
small bunch fresh basil

■ Heat the oil in a large, heavy-based saucepan. Fry the onion, garlic and celery for 5–10 minutes, until beginning to brown. Add the carrots and cook for a further 5 minutes.

■ Blend one can of cannellini beans with 300 ml/½ pint of vegetable stock. Stir in the whole beans, chopped tomatoes, tomato purée and remaining vegetable stock and bring to the boil. Reduce the heat and simmer for about 30 minutes, until all the vegetables are tender. Stir in the pesto, making sure it is evenly distributed. Season to taste.

■ Serve the soup hot, sprinkled with Parmesan cheese (omit for vegans) and garnished with basil, with warm, crusty French bread.

Serves 4

Opposite: Soupe au pistou

BAKED AVOCADOS
WITH STILTON

Strong blue Stilton cheese and creamy avocado are a classic combination. If Stilton is not to your taste, try a tasty Lancashire instead. These baked avocados are rich and filling as a main course for four people or would serve eight as a starter.

4 medium ripe avocados
1 tablespoon lemon juice
2 ripe plum tomatoes, skinned and chopped (or use canned)
100 g/4 oz vegetarian blue Stilton, crumbled
25 g/1 oz pine nuts, lightly toasted
few sprigs of basil leaves, torn
salt and freshly ground black pepper

Vinaigrette:
2 tablespoons extra virgin olive oil
1 tablespoon lemon juice
salt and freshly ground black pepper

To garnish:
250 g/9 oz packet mixed herb salad leaves
pine nuts
few basil leaves

■ Preheat the oven to 190°C/375°F/Gas Mark 5.
■ Halve the avocados, remove the stones and brush a little lemon juice over the cut surfaces to stop them discolouring.
■ Mix the chopped tomatoes, Stilton, pine nuts and basil together. Season with salt and pepper and fill each avocado half with the mixture.
■ Place in an ovenproof dish and bake in the preheated oven for 10–15 minutes.
■ Meanwhile, make the vinaigrette by mixing the olive oil and lemon juice together. Blend and season well with salt and pepper.
■ Serve immediately, surrounded by mixed herb salad leaves, drizzled with vinaigrette and garnished with pine nuts and basil leaves.

Serves 4

CHILLED MARINATED
MUSHROOMS

This recipe needs to be prepared in advance to give the flavours time to develop. It is good served as a starter with crusty bread, or you can make half the quantity and serve it as part of an antipasto platter or as one of a variety of salads.

2 red peppers
4 tablespoons olive oil
2 onions, chopped
2 garlic cloves, crushed
2.5-cm/1-in piece fresh ginger root, grated
2 tablespoons tomato purée
4 whole cloves
150 ml/¼ pint white wine
2 tablespoons soft brown sugar
900 g/2 lb button mushrooms
2–3 tablespoons shoyu
salt and freshly ground black pepper

■ Preheat the oven to 200°C/400°F/Gas Mark 6.
■ Put the red peppers on a baking sheet and cook in the preheated oven until the skins are blackening. Remove from the oven, place in a plastic bag and, when cool enough to handle, remove the skin and seeds, and slice thinly. Set aside and reserve the juices.
■ Heat the olive oil in a heavy-based saucepan. Fry the onions, garlic and ginger until colouring. Stir in the tomato purée, cloves, white wine and sugar. Bring to the boil, then reduce the heat and simmer for 15 minutes, until the sauce is thick. Add the mushrooms and cook for a further 5 minutes.
■ Take off the heat, season with shoyu and salt and pepper and add the red pepper strips and reserved juices. Cover and, when cold, chill. Serve cold with a rice salad or crusty bread to soak up the marinade.

Serves 4

SUITABLE FOR VEGANS

TIP
■
To make fresh ginger easier to grate, pare off the thin peel and freeze the ginger root. Grate from frozen. Fresh ginger keeps well in the fridge (about six weeks) or if you pot some up and keep it on your window sill you can grow your own and dig it up when you need it.

*CAN BE VEGAN

DEEP-FRIED POTATO
SKINS WITH TANGY DIPS

A popular supper dish, the potatoes can be cooked in advance and deep-fried at the last minute. If you don't have time to prepare the dips (which can also be made in advance and chilled), there are plenty to choose from 'off the shelf' in the supermarket!

8 large baking potatoes
2 tablespoons olive oil
salt
groundnut oil, for deep-frying

Honey mustard dip:
2 tablespoons white wine vinegar
2 tablespoons whole-grain mustard
2 tablespoons runny honey or
　maple syrup*
8 tablespoons olive oil

salt and freshly ground black pepper

Tangy tomato dip:
225 g /8 oz ripe tomatoes, skinned,
　deseeded and finely chopped
2 spring onions, finely chopped
½ bunch fresh coriander, chopped
1 teaspoon tabasco sauce
1 teaspoon balsamic vinegar
salt and freshly ground black
　pepper

■ Preheat the oven to 200°C/400°F/Gas Mark 6.
■ Scrub the potatoes, prick the skins and then brush with olive oil and sprinkle with salt. Place on a baking sheet and bake for about 50–60 minutes in the preheated oven, until tender when pierced with a fork.
■ Meanwhile, make the dips. For the honey mustard dip, mix together the vinegar, mustard and honey or maple syrup, then whisk in the olive oil, a tablespoon at a time, until thick and creamy. Season to taste.
■ For the tangy tomato dip, mix all the ingredients together and season to taste with salt and pepper.
■ When the potatoes are cooked, cut them in half lengthways and use a teaspoon to scoop out most of the flesh, leaving a layer of potato about 1 cm/½ in thick attached to the skin. Cut in half lengthways again.
■ Heat the groundnut oil in a wok. (The oil is hot enough when a small cube of bread dropped in sinks to the bottom, then immediately rises to the top, sizzling.)
■ Deep fry the potato skins, a few at a time, for about 1–2 minutes, until golden and crisp. Drain on kitchen paper and keep warm. When they are all cooked, sprinkle with salt and serve with the dips.

Serves 4

ALTERNATIVE DIPS

■

Tasty tartare
Mix 100 ml/4 fl oz crème fraîche with the juice of a lime, 1 tablespoon each of finely chopped capers and finely chopped gherkins, 1 crushed garlic clove and a handful of freshly chopped basil. Season to taste.

Olive dip
Chop 2 tablespoons green olives very finely and mix with 3 tablespoons olive oil, 1 tablespoon lemon juice and a handful of freshly chopped coriander. Season to taste.

Spicy mayo dip
Mix together 6 tablespoons vegetarian or vegan mayonnaise, 1 tablespoon mango chutney and 1 teaspoon of medium curry powder.

INDIVIDUAL
ARTICHOKE TARTS

*CAN BE VEGAN

A melt-in-the-mouth, very simple pastry that requires no rolling is combined with summery vegetables in these delicious little tarts. The balsamic vinegar sprinkled over the hot vegetables on serving brings out the flavour.

100 g /4 oz plain white flour
50 g /2 oz semolina
50 g /2 oz ground almonds
pinch of salt
100 g /4 oz butter or vegan margarine*
1 tablespoon cold water
4 teaspoons balsamic vinegar
basil leaves, to garnish

Artichoke filling:
2 tablespoons olive oil

100 g /4 oz red onions, halved
  and sliced
1 garlic clove, crushed
425 g /15 oz can artichoke hearts,
  drained and halved
2 spring onions, finely chopped
12 kalamata olives, stoned and
  finely chopped
100 g /4 oz cherry tomatoes, halved
salt and freshly ground black
  pepper

TIP

■

Fresh coriander also complements the flavour of artichokes and olives and may be used in place of the basil. A pinch of cayenne in the pastry also adds a little 'kick'.

■ Preheat the oven to 220°C/425°F/Gas Mark 7.
■ Mix the flour, semolina, ground almonds and salt in a bowl. Melt the butter or vegan margarine* with the water in a small saucepan. Pour into the dry ingredients and mix thoroughly to make a dough. Divide the dough into 4 pieces. Mould into four 10-cm/4-in loose-bottomed flan tins. Chill in the refrigerator for 30 minutes.
■ To make the filling, heat the oil and gently fry the red onions and garlic. Take off the heat and stir in all the other ingredients. Season well.
■ Spoon the filling into the flan cases and bake in the preheated oven for about 20–25 minutes, until the pastry is cooked and the vegetables are starting to char.
■ Turn out onto individual plates and sprinkle the vegetables with a little balsamic vinegar. Garnish with the basil leaves and serve.

Serves 4

*CAN BE VEGAN

ROAST VEGETABLE
AND SMOKED TOFU PLAIT

This is a lovely use of smoked tofu which is now readily available on the supermarket shelves. Smoked garlic is also easier to find and adds to the smoky flavour.

1 medium courgette, sliced
1 medium aubergine, cut into 1-cm/½-in cubes
1 red pepper, cut into 1-cm/½-in cubes
225 g/8 oz shallots, peeled and cut in half
8 smoked garlic cloves, peeled and left whole
225 g/8 oz smoked tofu, cut into small cubes
4 tablespoons olive oil
salt and freshly ground black pepper
2 tablespoons pine nuts
450 g/1 lb puff pastry, thawed if frozen
flour for rolling out
1 free-range egg, lightly beaten, or 1 tablespoon soya flour and
    2 tablespoons water*
sesame or poppy seeds, to decorate

■ Preheat the oven to 200°C/400°F/Gas Mark 6.
■ Arrange the vegetables on a baking tray together with the smoked tofu. Drizzle with olive oil and bake in the preheated oven until the vegetables are tender and starting to char slightly. Season and leave to cool.
■ Gently toast the pine nuts under a hot grill until golden. Mix into the vegetables.
■ Roll out the pastry, 225 g/8 oz at a time on a floured surface, to an oblong 20 × 32 cm/8 × 13 in) and place on a greased baking tray. Arrange half the vegetable filling down the centre of each piece. Cut strips 1 cm/½ in wide on either side of the filling, leaving 1 cm/½ in uncut on either side of the filling. Bring alternate strips over to enclose the filling, securing with egg wash or soya flour paste*.
■ Brush the top of the pastry with egg wash or soya paste* and decorate with sesame or poppy seeds. Bake in the preheated oven for 20–25 minutes, until crisp, well risen and golden.

Serves 4

TIP

■

If you prefer, you could use marinated tofu in place of smoked, or, for a non-vegan version, you could leave out the tofu and top the vegetables with pieces of vegetarian Brie just before enclosing the filling in the pastry.

Opposite: Roast vegetable and smoked tofu plait

CHEESY AUBERGINE
FILO PIE

Rich, cheesy and filling, this unusual pie has a slightly smoky flavour because the aubergines are baked. Make sure you prick them thoroughly all over with a fork or they will burst in the oven.

2 aubergines
2 tablespoons olive oil
25 g / 1 oz butter
25 g / 1 oz plain white flour
300–450 ml / 1/2 – 3/4 pint milk
50 g / 2 oz mozzarella cheese, cut into cubes
75 g / 3 oz vegetarian Cheddar cheese, grated
1 free-range egg, beaten

salt and freshly ground black pepper
pinch of nutmeg
225 g / 8 oz filo pastry
olive oil, for brushing

For the topping:
25 g / 1 oz vegetarian Cheddar cheese, grated
3 tablespoons breadcrumbs

■ Preheat the oven to 180°C/350°F/Gas Mark 4.
■ Wash and dry the aubergines and prick them all over with a fork. Place on a baking sheet and cook in the preheated oven for about 1 hour, turning several times. When tender, scoop out the flesh into a sieve and press lightly to extract the bitter juices. Chop the flesh roughly.
■ Make a white sauce. Melt the butter in a saucepan, add the flour and cook gently for 2–3 minutes, stirring all the time, to make a roux. Take the saucepan off the heat and add half of the milk, a little at a time, stirring constantly. Return to the heat, bring to the boil and simmer to thicken — if too thick, add more milk. When the desired consistency is reached, remove from the heat and stir in the mozzarella and Cheddar cheeses, beaten egg and chopped aubergine flesh. Season to taste with salt, pepper and nutmeg.
■ Unroll the filo pastry and cut to fit a greased 18-cm/7-in square cake tin. Keeping the unused pastry covered until needed, brush one sheet with olive oil and place in the base of the tin. Repeat with two more oiled sheets. Put half the cheese and aubergine mixture on top of the pastry. Brush three more sheets of pastry and place on top. Cover with the rest of the cheese and aubergine mixture. Finish with three more sheets of oiled filo pastry.
■ Mix the Cheddar and breadcrumbs together for the topping, and sprinkle over the top. Bake for about 1 hour, or until golden and set. Serve hot or at room temperature with a fresh green salad.

Serves 4

TIP
■

It is worth taking the time to make a roux-based white sauce, as cooking the fat and flour together removes the raw taste that an 'all-in-one' method tends to have. If you add the milk gradually, beating all the time, the sauce will be smooth. If disaster strikes, pop it into a blender and blend for a few seconds – the lumps will disappear.

SAVOURY PANCAKES
WITH ROAST VEGETABLE FILLING

SUITABLE FOR
VEGANS

The pancakes can be made in advance, then stacked with sheets of greaseproof paper in between and frozen until required.

1 courgette, cut into 1-cm/½-in cubes
1 aubergine, cut into 1-cm/½-in cubes
8 shallots or small onions,
    quartered
8 garlic cloves, peeled and left whole
1 head fennel, cut into 1-cm/½-in
    pieces
1 red or yellow pepper, cut into
    1-cm/½-in cubes
salt and freshly ground black
    pepper
4 tablespoons olive oil
1 tablespoon chopped fresh parsley
chopped fresh parsley, to garnish

Savoury pancakes:
50 g/2 oz plain white flour
50 g/2 oz gram (chick pea) flour, sieved
300 ml/½ pint soya milk
1 teaspoon groundnut oil

Tomato sauce:
1 tablespoon olive oil
1 onion, finely chopped
1 garlic clove, crushed
425-g/15-oz can chopped tomatoes
1 tablespoon red wine vinegar
1 tablespoon soft brown sugar
salt and freshly ground black pepper

> **TIP**
> ■
> The variations on savoury pancakes are endless. Try adding a pinch of cumin and coriander to the pancake batter and fill the pancakes with your favourite vegetarian curry, omitting the tomato sauce and covering with foil before baking; or for a wintery dish, try a mixture of roasted root vegetables, such as butternut squash, carrots, parsnips, sweet potato and shallots, in place of the 'Mediterranean' vegetables in this recipe.

■ Preheat the oven to 200°C/400°F/Gas Mark 6.

■ Place the prepared vegetables in a roasting pan. Season with salt and pepper and toss in olive oil. Roast in the preheated oven for 30–40 minutes, until golden. Remove from the oven, cool and stir in the chopped parsley. Reduce the oven temperature to 180°C/350°F/Gas Mark 4.

■ Make the pancake batter. Blend the flours and soya milk together and leave to stand for 20 minutes.

■ Meanwhile, make the sauce. Heat the oil in a heavy-based saucepan, and fry the onion and garlic until soft. Add the tomatoes, vinegar, sugar and seasoning to taste. Remove from the heat and set aside.

■ Heat the groundnut oil for the pancakes in an 18-cm/7-in non-stick frying pan. When really hot, pour in enough batter to thinly coat the pan. Cook over a moderate heat until the underside of the pancake is brown, turn over and cook the other side. Make 8 pancakes in total.

■ Place one pancake in a large greased ovenproof dish. Put some of the roasted vegetable filling in the centre and roll up. Repeat with the remaining pancakes and pack neatly into the dish. Cover with tomato sauce and bake in the oven for 30 minutes, until heated through. Serve garnished with parsley.

Serves 4

SUITABLE FOR
VEGANS

EXOTIC VEGETABLE
STIR-FRY

The secret of making a crisp and delicious stir-fry is to prepare all the ingredients before you start cooking, to keep the oil hot and to cook those vegetables that will take the longest first.

TIP

■

To make fresh ginger juice, peel a 5-cm/2-in piece of fresh root ginger, then grate it and squeeze the juice out of the grated flesh. To extract the maximum amount of juice, put the flesh into a garlic press and squeeze — the juice will come through the holes, leaving the fibrous flesh behind.

2 tablespoons groundnut oil
I red onion, cut in half and sliced
I garlic clove, crushed
100 g/4 oz fresh shiitake mushrooms, stalks removed and sliced
I red chilli, deseeded and finely chopped
2 baby aubergines, quartered
5-cm/2-in piece mooli, cut into thin circles
50 g/2 oz baby carrots, halved lengthways
50 g/2 oz baby sweetcorn, halved
50 g/2 oz mange tout, topped, tailed and halved

50 g/2 oz green beans, cut into 2.5-cm/1-in pieces
100 g/4 oz baby spinach leaves, washed

Szechuan sauce:
I teaspoon fresh ginger juice
I tablespoon shoyu
I tablespoon lime juice
I teaspoon szechuan pepper, ground

To serve:
225 g/8 oz white long-grain rice, boiled
2 spring onions, shredded or tassled
few sprigs of fresh coriander

■ Heat the oil in a wok. When really hot, add the red onion and garlic and fry for 2 minutes. Add the shiitake mushrooms and chilli and cook for 3 minutes. Then add the baby aubergines and cook for 5 minutes, stirring and tossing the vegetables all the time.

■ Add the mooli, carrots and sweetcorn and cook for 3 minutes, then the mange tout and green beans and cook for a further 3 minutes. Finally, add the baby spinach leaves. Stir and cook until wilted.

■ Mix together the sauce ingredients and toss into the stir-fried vegetables. Serve on a bed of boiled rice, garnished with spring onions and coriander.

Serves 4

MARINATED SPICED
AUBERGINES

Aubergines and tomatoes are a classic flavour combination and the spicy marinade complements the vegetables. This would also make a good dish cooked on your barbecue.

7 tablespoons olive oil
2 garlic cloves, crushed
$\frac{1}{2}$ teaspoon ground coriander
$\frac{1}{2}$ teaspoon ground cumin
$\frac{1}{4}$–$\frac{1}{2}$ teaspoon chilli powder
salt and freshly ground black pepper
2 medium aubergines, each sliced
   into four lengthways

$\frac{1}{2}$ teaspoon whole coriander seeds,
   lightly crushed
$\frac{1}{2}$ teaspoon whole cumin seeds,
   lightly crushed
1 onion, sliced
450 g / 1 lb ripe tomatoes, skinned
   and sliced
crusty bread, to serve

■ Preheat the oven to 190°C/375°F/Gas Mark 5.
■ Mix 6 tablespoons of the olive oil with one of the crushed garlic cloves. Add the ground spices and season with salt and pepper.
■ Brush both sides of each aubergine slice with the seasoned oil. Lay the slices in a shallow dish, pour over any remaining marinade and cover. Leave to marinate for 30–60 minutes.
■ Heat the remaining olive oil in a saucepan and gently fry the coriander and cumin seeds for a few seconds. Add the onion and remaining garlic and cook until golden brown. Add the tomatoes and cook for 5 minutes. Season to taste with salt and pepper and then set aside.
■ Grill the marinated aubergines until cooked on both sides (or cook on a griddle pan to give the aubergines charred stripes). Place the grilled aubergines in a shallow ovenproof dish or roasting pan.
■ Reheat the tomato and onion mixture and spread over the aubergines. Heat through in the preheated oven for about 20 minutes. Serve hot with plenty of crusty bread.

Serves 4

TIP
■

At one time aubergines needed to be 'degorged' by sprinkling the cut surfaces with salt to draw out the bitter juices. Modern varieties are much less bitter and it is no longer necessary to do this. These aubergines could be served as part of an Indian meal with Naan Bread, or with a bulgar wheat salad. Just mix 225 g/8 oz soaked bulgar wheat with some finely chopped cucumber and 3 skinned and chopped tomatoes. Add a handful of chopped fresh herbs of your choice, mix with a classic vinaigrette and season well.

PASTA WITH LEEKS IN A TARRAGON CREAM SAUCE

This pasta dish is extremely quick to make and ideal for an informal meal with friends. The sauce can be cooked at the same time as the pasta and the whole process takes less than 20 minutes.

225 g/8 oz conchiglie (pasta shells)
25 g/1 oz butter or vegan margarine*
225 g/8 oz leeks, trimmed and finely shredded
1 garlic clove, crushed
12 g/½ oz dried ceps (porcini), soaked in warm water for about 15 minutes
25 g/1 oz plain white flour
150 ml/¼ pint vegetable stock
150 ml/¼ pint vegetarian white wine
2 tablespoons chopped fresh tarragon
salt and freshly ground black pepper
3 tablespoons single cream or soya cream*

■ Cook the pasta in boiling lightly salted water according to the manufacturer's instructions. Drain well.
■ Meanwhile, make the sauce. Melt the butter or vegan margarine* in a large, heavy saucepan. Gently cook the leeks and garlic until tender. Drain the ceps, chop very finely and add to the pan.
■ Stir in the flour. Take the pan off the heat and gradually add the stock and white wine, stirring all the time to prevent lumps from forming.
■ Put the pan back on the heat, bring to the boil, then simmer for 5 minutes, until the sauce has thickened, stirring all the time.
■ Stir in the tarragon and seasoning to taste, and then add the cream or soya cream*.
■ Toss the cooked pasta into the sauce and serve immediately with garlic bread or a mixed green salad.

Serves 4

TIP
■

Pasta is a marvellous convenience food. If you have unexpected guests for supper you can quickly make a sauce with store cupboard ingredients. Just chop and fry an onion in olive oil, add a pinch of dried oregano, a can of chopped tomatoes and a can of drained flageolet beans. Serve on a bed of pasta with freshly grated vegetarian cheese. Your guests will be impressed with your versatility!

FARFALLE WITH
MUSHROOMS AND SPINACH

*CAN BE VEGAN

Versatile pasta can be used as the basis for many quick but satisfying meals. This speedy dish with its interesting vegetables is ideal for informal entertaining.

225 g/8 oz farfalle pasta

2 tablespoons olive oil

225 g/8 oz mixed mushrooms, e.g. oyster, shiitake
    and field, thickly sliced

2 garlic cloves, crushed

100 g/4 oz baby spinach leaves, washed and dried

6 sun-dried tomatoes in oil, finely chopped

salt and freshly ground black pepper

To garnish:

$^1/_2$ bunch fresh basil leaves

100 g/4 oz cherry tomatoes, halved

- Cook the pasta in lightly salted boiling water as instructed on the packet.
- Meanwhile, heat the olive oil in a large frying pan. Quickly fry the mushrooms and garlic over a high heat for 2–3 minutes, until just cooked.
- Add the baby spinach leaves and stir until wilted. Stir in the sun-dried tomatoes and seasoning to taste.
- Drain the pasta and toss into the mushroom and spinach mixture. Turn into a serving dish, and serve garnished with torn fresh basil and cherry tomatoes.

Serves 4

TIP

■

A delicious addition to this recipe would be a tablespoon of (vegan) pesto, stirred in just before serving, and some toasted pine nuts sprinkled over the top. You can use different pasta shapes — the flat, ribbon-like tagliatelle works well with this mixture.

SUMMER
AND AL FRESCO ENTERTAINING

Left: Barbecue spread

BARBECUE MENU

■

Choose a selection from the following dishes to serve 4 people.

■

Spiced sweet potato slices

Beef tomatoes with balsamic vinegar marinade

Aubergine and Halloumi rolls

Peppers stuffed with tomatoes and feta cheese

Vegetable kebabs with oriental dressing

Tandoori-style paneer tikka kebabs

SUITABLE FOR VEGANS

SPICED SWEET
POTATO SLICES

You can vary the spice mixture used in this recipe to suit your own taste. It can also be brushed over raw slices of squash or aubergine and grilled in the same way.

2 large pink sweet potatoes, peeled and left whole
2 tablespoons olive oil
$1/2$ teaspoon ground coriander
$1/2$ teaspoon ground cumin
pinch of ground cardamom seeds
sea salt, to taste

■ Parboil the sweet potatoes for about 10 minutes, until just tender.
■ Allow to cool slightly and cut into 6-mm/$1/4$-in slices lengthways.
■ Mix the olive oil and spices together, brush them over the slices of sweet potato and then place over hot barbecue coals for a few minutes on each side until crisp and golden.
■ Sprinkle the spiced sweet potato slices with sea salt and serve immediately.

Serves 4

BEEF TOMATOES WITH
BALSAMIC VINEGAR MARINADE

SUITABLE
VEGANS

Easy, summery and Mediterranean, this dish uses the flavoursome large beef tomatoes. If you prefer, you could use smaller tomatoes straight from the garden, but reduce the cooking time a little.

4 ripe beef tomatoes
4 teaspoons balsamic vinegar
freshly ground black pepper
2 tablespoons olive oil
12 g / ½ oz fresh basil leaves
8 kalamata olives, to garnish

■ Cut the tomatoes in half, then make shallow criss-cross cuts over each cut side. Drizzle a little balsamic vinegar over each and season with black pepper. Leave to marinate for 30 minutes.

■ Brush both sides of each tomato half with olive oil, place skin-side down on the barbecue and grill gently until tender (about 10 minutes).

■ Sprinkle with extra balsamic vinegar, if liked, and scatter lots of torn fresh basil leaves over the top of each tomato. Chop the olives coarsely and scatter over the top of the tomatoes.

Serves 4

TIP
■

An alternative and very tasty marinade is to mix together 2 tablespoons of sunflower oil, 1 teaspoon of chilli oil (or 2 small dried chillies, crushed), 1 tablespoon of shoyu, 1 crushed garlic clove and 1 teaspoon of grated ginger. Season with black pepper. Make shallow criss-cross cuts on the tomato halves and drizzle over as before. Or mix a little honey, oil and lemon juice together and brush over the tomato halves. The sweetness of the honey brings out the flavour of the tomato.

Aubergine and Halloumi Rolls

This recipe or variations on it have been appearing on my barbecue for years. It now seems to be becoming a popular dish for all the TV cooks as well — so you know it's going to be good! The rolls can also be cooked easily on a conventional grill and served as a starter or finger food.

1 large aubergine
salt, for sprinkling
150 ml/¼ pint olive oil
freshly ground black pepper
8 teaspoons sun-dried tomato paste
8 basil leaves
225 g/8 oz Halloumi, cut into 8 pieces
16 wooden cocktail sticks, soaked in water for 30 minutes

■ Trim the end and slice the aubergine into 8 thin slices lengthways. Place on a baking tray and sprinkle with salt. Leave for 30–60 minutes, until the bitter juices have been extracted and the slices are pliable. Rinse the aubergine slices well and pat dry with kitchen paper.

■ Season the olive oil with freshly ground black pepper and brush over one side of each aubergine slice. Spread 1 teaspoon of sun-dried tomato paste over each slice, then place a basil leaf topped with a piece of Halloumi on one end of the aubergine slice and roll up. Secure by skewering with 2 criss-crossed cocktail sticks.

■ Brush the outside of the aubergine rolls with olive oil and barbecue for about 5–6 minutes on each side, until tender and starting to char.

Serves 4

BARBECUES FOR

BARBECUE TIPS

■

If you are using a 'traditional' barbecue, allow at least 30–45 minutes for the coals to become really hot before starting to cook. A gas barbecue is quicker but takes away some of the fun!

Buy long metal skewers for kebabs so that the handle ends are not over the coals and are easier to turn.

Long-handled tongs are useful for turning food, and a pair of oven gloves will stop you burning yourself when handling hot utensils.

PEPPERS STUFFED WITH
TOMATOES AND FETA CHEESE

Peppers, tomatoes and basil all complement each other. You can use sliced salad tomatoes in place of the sun-dried ones in this recipe, and ciabatta bread is wonderful for soaking up the juices.

4 red peppers
8 sun-dried tomatoes in oil
12 g / ½ oz fresh basil leaves, roughly torn
225 g / 8 oz feta cheese in oil
olive oil to drizzle
salt and freshly ground black pepper

- Halve the peppers lengthways through the stalk and remove the seeds.
- Place 1 sun-dried tomato in each half and sprinkle with half of the torn basil, reserving the rest for the garnish. Top with pieces of feta cheese.
- Drizzle each one with olive oil or a little of the oil from the tomatoes and cheese. Season with salt and freshly ground black pepper.
- Grill the stuffed peppers on the barbecue for about 10-15 minutes, until the peppers are cooked, the skin is charred and the cheese is starting to melt.
- Garnish with the reserved torn basil and serve with crusty garlic bread or bulgar wheat to soak up the juice.

Serves 4

TIP
■

Salads complement barbecue food and, if fairly substantial, give your guests something to eat while the rest of the food is cooking. Try a tabbouleh (bulgar wheat salad), or quinoa with grilled courgettes and a minty vinaigrette and crumbled feta cheese. Pasta salads with lots of chopped, fresh vegetables and a vegan mayonnaise work well too. You can also cook some garlic bread in a foil parcel on the barbecue. Hand this round with the salad and use to soak up the marinade juices.

VEGETABLE KEBABS
WITH ORIENTAL DRESSING

TIP

■

These kebabs are also
good served with the
satay sauce on page 93.

This recipe is dairy free, but a delicious variation is to add
225 g/8 oz Halloumi cheese, cut into chunks and threaded onto
the skewers between the vegetables. Barbecues always seem to
involve a great deal of preparation, so to make things simpler, use one
of the ready flavoured packets of rice as an accompaniment — if you
feel you have time, you can make your own if you prefer.

1 medium courgette, cut into 16 slices
4 small onions or shallots, peeled
    and halved
1 yellow or orange pepper, deseeded
    and cut into 8 pieces
8 button mushrooms
4 cherry tomatoes
4 x 20-cm/8-in wooden skewers,
    soaked in water for 30 minutes
4 tablespoons olive oil
salt and freshly ground black pepper

Oriental dressing:
1 tablespoon shoyu

3 tablespoons cold-pressed
    sunflower oil
1 teaspoon fresh ginger juice (grate
    and squeeze juice out)
1 garlic clove, crushed
1 teaspoon toasted sesame oil
2 tablespoons fresh lime juice (or
    lemon if preferred)
salt and freshly ground black
    pepper

To serve:
225 g/8 oz ready flavoured Thai rice,
    cooked and chilled

■ Thread all the vegetables onto the wooden skewers, brush with olive oil
and season with salt and pepper. Grill over hot barbecue coals for about
10–15 minutes, turning frequently, until golden and tender.
■ Meanwhile, make the oriental dressing by beating all the ingredients
together and seasoning to taste.
■ Pour the dressing over the hot kebabs and serve with the chilled rice 'salad'.

Serves 4

TANDOORI-STYLE
PANEER TIKKA KEBABS

It is unusual to have a tandoori flavour in a vegetarian meal. Paneer is a firm Indian cheese which soaks up the flavour of the marinade and keeps its shape when cooked. This recipe is wonderful on a barbecue, but can also be cooked under a conventional grill if the weather changes. It makes a good starter for an Indian meal (see the Indian dinner party on page 97) or you can make smaller portions on cocktail sticks for party finger food.

150 ml/5 fl oz natural yogurt
juice of ½ lemon
1 tablespoon tandoori spice mix
200 g/7 oz paneer, cut into 24 cubes
1 green pepper, deseeded and cut
    into 16 pieces
8 small onions or shallots, peeled
    and halved
4 cherry tomatoes, halved

8 x 15-cm/6-in wooden skewers,
    soaked in water for 30 minutes
2 tablespoons groundnut oil

To serve:
4 pappads
shredded lettuce
cucumber and tomato slices
lemon quarters

> **TIP**
> ■
> Pappads are similar to poppadums, but are usually smaller and can be grilled for about a minute on each side until they puff up, unlike poppadums which are often deep fried and oilier. Both pappads and poppadums are sold in most supermarkets. If you have a microwave oven, they can be cooked in this way instead.

■ Mix the yogurt, lemon juice and tandoori spice mix together in a shallow bowl. Add the cubes of paneer and stir to coat thoroughly. Cover and leave to marinate for 30–60 minutes (or overnight) in the refrigerator.

■ Thread the green pepper, paneer, onions and tomatoes onto each skewer. Brush with groundnut oil, place over hot coals and grill, turning frequently, until the vegetables and cheese are cooked and starting to char.

■ Grill the pappads as per the instructions on the packet. Serve the kebabs with the salad garnish, lemon quarters and pappads.

Serves 4

PICNIC MENU

■

Choose a selection from the following dishes to serve 4 people.

■

Aubergine, courgette and tomato cob

Crostini

Mint and butter bean pâté

Roast vegetables and goat's cheese en croûte

Savoury tomato and basil tatin

SUITABLE FOR VEGANS

TIP

■

You can vary the filling in this cob by adding a layer of roasted peppers, a selection of quickly fried exotic mushrooms, some wilted spinach or slices of mozzarella or feta cheese.

AUBERGINE,
COURGETTE AND TOMATO COB

This stuffed cob holds together to make a really colourful savoury 'gâteau' when cut into wedges. It is excellent for picnics as it is easy to transport and keeps its shape.

1 white, round, crusty loaf, e.g. pain de campagne, or 4 individual crusty rolls
1 aubergine, sliced
3 tablespoons olive oil
1 large onion, sliced
2 garlic cloves, crushed
1 tablespoon brown sugar
225 g /8 oz courgettes, sliced
4 ripe tomatoes, skinned and sliced
1 tablespoon chopped fresh basil
1 tablespoon chopped fresh flat-leaf parsley
1 tablespoon chopped fresh oregano
salt and freshly ground black pepper

■ Preheat the oven to 200°C/400°F/Gas Mark 6.
■ Slice the top off the loaf or rolls and reserve. Remove the bread from the inside, leaving just a shell.
■ Brush the aubergine slices with a little of the olive oil, place on a baking sheet and bake in the preheated oven for about 15-20 minutes, until golden.
■ Heat the remaining olive oil in a frying pan. Fry the onion and garlic gently for about 15 minutes, until turning golden and starting to caramelize. Stir in the sugar and remove from the pan.
■ In the same pan, add a little more olive oil if necessary and fry the courgettes until golden.
■ Layer half the aubergine, onion, courgettes, tomatoes and half the herbs inside the bread shell, seasoning each layer. Repeat the layers and put the lid on top. Wrap tightly in cling film and refrigerate for 2 hours or overnight. The juices will soak into the bread. Cut into wedges to serve.

Serves 4

Opposite: Aubergine, courgette and tomato cob

CROSTINI

TIP

■

Although this recipe uses ciabatta bread, you could just as easily use thin slices of French stick prepared in the same way. If you don't like the flavour of raw garlic omit this from the recipe. The toppings given in this recipe are all cold and are therefore suitable for a picnic, but to make a change, add a little vegetarian mozzarella or Cheddar and pop them under the grill. Serve as appetizers when you are entertaining at home.

Crostini are small slices of bread, brushed with olive oil, toasted and topped with all manner of ingredients — the variety is as great as your imagination. All the elements of this recipe can be made 24 hours in advance.

12 slices day-old ciabatta bread
4–6 tablespoons olive oil
1 garlic clove, skinned and left whole

Mushroom topping:
50 g/2 oz button mushrooms, sliced
1 tablespoon olive oil
1 teaspoon herb vinegar
1 teaspoon mixed ground cumin
  and coriander
4 slices mozzarella cheese (omit
  for vegans*)

Mediterranean topping:
1/2 red onion, finely chopped

2 sun-dried tomatoes in oil, finely
  chopped
4 kalamata olives, stoned and
  chopped
1 teaspoon oregano, chopped
1 tablespoon olive oil
1 teaspoon balsamic vinegar
salt and freshly ground black pepper

Aubergine topping:
1 tablespoon olive oil
1/2 aubergine, finely chopped
2 ripe tomatoes, skinned and chopped
1 teaspoon basil leaves, torn
salt and freshly ground black pepper

■ Preheat the oven to 200°C/400°F/Gas Mark 6.
■ Brush each side of the slices of ciabatta bread with olive oil. Place on a baking tray and bake in the preheated oven for 10–25 minutes, until crisp and golden. Rub the clove of garlic over one side of each slice.
■ To make the mushroom topping, mix all the ingredients except the mozzarella together in a bowl. Leave to marinate for at least 30 minutes. Top 4 slices of the toast with the mixture and a slice of mozzarella cheese*, if using. Quickly melt the cheese under a hot grill before serving hot or cold.
■ For the Mediterranean topping, mix all the ingredients together and leave to marinate for at least 30 minutes. Use to top 4 slices of the toast.
■ For the aubergine topping, heat the olive oil in a pan and gently fry the aubergine until golden and tender. Stir in the tomatoes and basil and season to taste. Either top 4 slices of toast immediately and serve hot or, for a picnic, leave to cool and use the topping cold.

Serves 4

MINT AND BUTTER
BEAN PATE

Other pulses, such as flageolets, cannellini beans or canned broad beans, can be used in place of the butter beans in this delicious pâté. It can be turned into a dip by adding extra lemon juice and olive oil and a little tahini if liked (a variation on hummus). Serve with vegetable crudités (see page 74).

2 x 425-g/15-oz cans of butter beans, drained
grated zest and juice of 1 lemon
2 garlic cloves, crushed
2 tablespoons finely chopped fresh mint
4 tablespoons olive oil
4 tablespoons water (approx.)
salt and freshly ground black pepper
sprigs of mint, to garnish

To serve:
pitta bread triangles
mixed salad leaves and cherry tomatoes

■ Place the butter beans and lemon juice in a food processor and blend until smooth. Add the lemon zest, garlic, mint and olive oil, adjusting the amount of water to give a smooth pâté. Season to taste, then spoon the mixture into a serving dish or individual ramekins and garnish with mint sprigs.

■ Serve the butter bean pâté with warm pitta bread triangles and a salad garnish of lettuce and cherry tomatoes.

Serves 4

ROAST VEGETABLES
AND GOAT'S CHEESE EN CROUTE

The usual mixture of roast vegetables consists of roots, such as carrot, parsnip and sweet potato, or Mediterranean vegetables, such as aubergines and peppers. This recipe quickly roasts some of the more tender summer vegetables and uses the now popular goat's cheese to add extra flavour. If you find goat's cheese too strong, try using feta or even a crumbly Wensleydale instead.

100 g/4 oz baby courgettes, quartered
50 g/2 oz green beans, cut into 2.5-cm/1-in pieces
50 g/2 oz mange tout, topped, tailed and halved
50 g/2 oz fennel, chopped (optional)
50 g/2 oz cherry tomatoes, halved

8 spring onions, quartered
8 garlic cloves, peeled and left whole
few sprigs of fresh rosemary
4 tablespoons olive oil
225 g/8 oz puff pastry
100 g/4 oz goat's cheese, sliced
salt and freshly ground black pepper
1 free-range egg, beaten

■ Preheat the oven to 200°C/400°F/Gas Mark 6.

■ Place all the prepared vegetables, including the spring onions and garlic, in a baking dish, together with the rosemary. Toss in the olive oil and bake, turning frequently, in the preheated oven for about 20 minutes, until starting to colour.

■ Remove from the oven and allow to cool. Remove the rosemary sprigs.

■ Roll out the puff pastry to make a square, 30 × 30 cm/12 × 12 in, and cut into 4 equal pieces, 15 × 15 cm/6 × 6 in. Place a quarter of the vegetable mixture on each pastry square. Top with the goat's cheese and season to taste.

■ Brush the edges of the pastry with egg and fold over into a triangle. Seal the edges well. Make a slit in the top of each package, and place on a baking tray. Brush with egg to glaze and bake in the preheated oven for about 20 minutes, until risen and golden. Serve warm or cold.

Serves 4

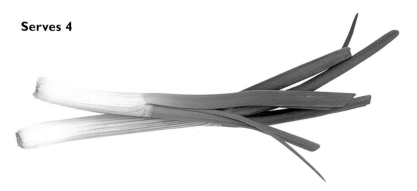

SAVOURY TOMATO
AND BASIL TATIN

These upside-down tarts were originally created by the Tatin sisters in France using caramelized apples topped with a rich pastry. The idea has become deservedly popular as it gives a lovely crisp pastry top which, when inverted, becomes the base. Try to get the sweet yellow cherry tomatoes for this recipe as they make an interesting contrast to the red.

200 g/7 oz plain flour
pinch of salt
100 g/4 oz vegan margarine
1 teaspoon dried basil
4–6 olives, finely chopped
4–6 tablespoons cold water
225 g/8 oz onions, sliced
1 tablespoon olive oil

450 g/1 lb ripe, flavoursome
    tomatoes, e.g. plum or beef, sliced
225 g/8 oz yellow (or red) cherry
    tomatoes, halved
1 bunch fresh basil
salt and freshly ground black pepper
few olives, halved
basil leaves, to garnish

- Preheat the oven to 200°C/400°F/Gas Mark 6.
- Sift the flour and salt into a bowl. Rub in the margarine to resemble breadcrumbs. Stir in the basil and olives and enough water to make a firm dough. Roll into a ball, wrap in cling film and chill for 30 minutes.
- Meanwhile, fry the onions in the olive oil until starting to brown, then remove from the heat and allow to cool.
- Arrange the tomato slices and cherry tomato halves, cut-side down, in a decorative way on the base of a 20-cm/8-in solid-based cake tin. Reserve some of the basil leaves for the garnish and roughly tear the rest and sprinkle over the tomatoes. Season with salt and pepper and top with the onions.

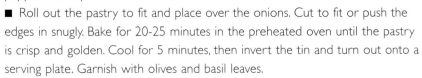

- Roll out the pastry to fit and place over the onions. Cut to fit or push the edges in snugly. Bake for 20-25 minutes in the preheated oven until the pastry is crisp and golden. Cool for 5 minutes, then invert the tin and turn out onto a serving plate. Garnish with olives and basil leaves.

Serves 6

PICNIC TIPS
■

Try to provide food that can be eaten without knives and forks and which doesn't collapse between plate and mouth.

Over- rather than underestimate the food for a picnic — the fresh air always seems to sharpen the appetite and everyone will eat more than normal!

**SUITABLE FOR
VEGANS**

SUSHI

It is now much easier to obtain Japanese ingredients and these chilled sushi make a light and summery starter. Watch out for the wasabi paste — it is much hotter than our native horseradish!

100 g/4 oz Arborio or other short-
   grain rice
2 teaspoons wasabi paste
4 tablespoons shoyu
a few pieces chopped, pickled ginger

Avocado filling:
½ avocado, peeled and sliced
1 tablespoon lemon juice
1 sheet nori (sea vegetable), toasted
   and cut into 1.25-cm/½-in strips
1 teaspoon wasabi paste (Japanese
   horseradish paste)

Red pepper filling:
1 sheet nori, toasted
1 tablespoon umeboshi sauce (plum)
¼ red pepper, cut into thin strips
2.5-cm/1-in piece cucumber, cut into
   matchsticks

Ginger filling:
4 capers, finely chopped
few sprigs of fresh mint, finely
   chopped
16–20 slices pickled ginger in rice
   wine vinegar

■ Cook the rice in boiling water, stirring occasionally to release the starch and make the rice sticky. Drain and cool until needed.

■ For the avocado filling, take one-third of the cooked rice and form into 4 cubes. Toss the avocado slices in the lemon juice to stop them discolouring. Toast the nori over a gas flame for a few seconds, until it becomes green and translucent. Cut into strips. Take a cube of rice, put a little wasabi on top, then a slice of avocado and tie in place with a strip of nori. Chill.

■ For the red pepper filling, place the toasted nori on a sushi mat or piece of cling film. Spread one-third of the rice over the nori. Make an indentation 1.25–2.5 cm/½–1 in in from one long edge with a chop stick, and spread with a little umeboshi sauce. Place the pepper and cucumber strips side by side along the indentation. Roll up firmly, using the mat or cling film to help you. Chill and cut into slices.

■ For the ginger filling, take the remaining cooked rice and mix in the capers and fresh mint. Lay 4-5 pieces of pickled ginger onto a piece of cling film, put a heaped tablespoon of the rice mixture in the centre and bring the ginger up around to enclose it. Use the cling film to compress the ball by gathering tightly and twisting. Refrigerate until ready to serve. Repeat 3 more times.

■ To serve: arrange a selection of sushi on each plate with ½ teaspoon of wasabi paste, a small bowl containing 1 tablespoon of shoyu and a little pile of chopped pickled ginger.

Opposite: Sushi

COUS COUS
WITH SUMMER VEGETABLES

During the summer months it is wonderful to be able to use the new produce when it is young, crisp and full of flavour — much better than the woody or watery vegetables that are found on the supermarket shelves when they are full grown. This recipe makes full use of these delightful vegetables and the cous cous absorbs the flavour of the dressing.

225 g/8 oz cous cous
100 g/4 oz baby carrots, topped
and tailed
100 g/4 oz baby courgettes, topped,
tailed and halved
100 g/4 oz mange tout, topped, tailed
and halved
4 tablespoons olive oil
8 shallots or small onions, quartered

I stick celery, sliced
2 tablespoons white wine vinegar
grated zest of I lemon
I tablespoon chopped fresh
coriander
salt and freshly ground black pepper
100 g/4 oz cherry tomatoes
25 g/I oz pine nuts, toasted
coriander leaves, to garnish

∎ Place the cous cous in a bowl. Pour boiling water over and leave to stand for 15 minutes. Drain off any excess water, cool and spoon into a serving dish.
∎ Steam the baby carrots, courgettes and mange tout until just tender. Put 1 tablespoon of the olive oil in a saucepan and quickly fry the shallots or baby onions until golden brown. Add the celery and cook for 2 minutes. Remove from the heat and allow to cool.
∎ Mix the remaining olive oil with the vinegar and lemon zest. Add the chopped coriander and season well.
∎ Mix all the vegetables and cherry tomatoes together, toss in the vinaigrette and spoon over the top of the cous cous. Top with the toasted pine nuts and serve garnished with coriander leaves.

BEANSPROUT SALAD
WITH SESAME DRESSING

This is a fresh and summery salad with an oriental touch. If you grow your own chives, use some of the edible flower heads for a pretty garnish; they make an interesting talking point.

½ head of Chinese leaves, finely shredded
100 g/4 oz baby spinach leaves, washed and coarsely chopped
100 g/4 oz beansprouts
4 spring onions, shredded
50 g/2 oz baby sweetcorn, halved lengthways
50 g/2 oz mange tout, topped, tailed and blanched

1 tablespoon sesame seeds
few chives, chopped, for garnish

For the dressing:
2 tablespoons rice wine vinegar
1 tablespoon sunflower or groundnut oil
1 teaspoon toasted sesame oil
salt and freshly ground black pepper

■ Prepare the Chinese leaves, spinach, beansprouts, spring onions, sweetcorn and mange tout, and mix together in a large bowl.
■ Mix the dressing ingredients together, then pour over the salad. Toss well and arrange on a large platter.
■ Dry toast the sesame seeds in a non-stick pan. Sprinkle over the top of the salad. Serve garnished with chopped chives.

TIP

Chinese bean sprouts are sprouted mung beans, but many other pulses and seeds can be sprouted successfully. Place about 2 tablespoons into a wide necked jar with muslin over the top. Rinse and drain thoroughly twice a day. Try green lentils or fenugreek seeds for a slightly spicy flavour, or alfalfa seeds for the fresh taste of baby peas.

SUMMER MENU 2
■
SERVES 4
■

Sweet and sour peppers

Lemony flageolet bean salad

Mixed tomato salad

Italian spinach and ricotta gnocchi

Nectarine and physalis cream pie
(see page 112)

*CAN BE VEGAN

SWEET AND SOUR
BAKED PEPPERS

The combination of vinegar and honey (or maple syrup) brings out the natural flavours of this dish. It can be eaten as an appetizer or a main dish, and can even be served on a bed of pasta.

5 tablespoons olive oil
1 large onion, sliced
2 garlic cloves, crushed
4 mixed colour peppers, deseeded and sliced
225 g/8 oz ripe tomatoes, skinned and chopped
2 tablespoons red wine vinegar
1 tablespoon honey or maple syrup*
1 tablespoon tomato purée
salt and freshly ground black pepper

To serve:
1 tablespoon balsamic vinegar
½ bunch fresh basil leaves, torn
12 olives, stoned and halved
crusty white bread

■ Preheat the oven to 200°C/400°F/Gas Mark 6.
■ Use one tablespoon of the olive oil to fry the onion and garlic until just soft. Mix in all the other ingredients, season and turn into an ovenproof dish.
■ Bake in the preheated oven for 40–50 minutes, basting occasionally, until the peppers are browning in patches. Remove from the oven and serve sprinkled with balsamic vinegar, freshly torn basil and olives, with crusty white bread.

LEMONY BEAN SALAD

This substantial salad can be served as a starter with crusty bread. It is also good for barbecues.

100 g/4 oz baby spinach leaves, washed

425 g/15 oz can flageolet beans, rinsed and drained

2 ripe avocados, peeled, stoned and sliced

1 red onion, finely chopped

1–2 tablespoons sunflower seeds

For the dressing:

juice and finely chopped zest of 1 lemon

2 tablespoons fruity extra virgin olive oil

apple juice concentrate, to taste

1 teaspoon Dijon mustard

salt and freshly ground black pepper

■ Arrange the baby spinach leaves on a platter. Mix the prepared flageolet beans, avocados and red onion together and arrange on top of the spinach.

■ Mix the dressing ingredients together and drizzle over the salad.

■ Dry toast the sunflower seeds in a pan and scatter over the top.

TIPS FOR SUMMER ENTERTAINING

■

Summer is always a good time of year for entertaining and it is a good idea to prepare as much as possible in advance and then serve it cold.

Keep the cooking simple to avoid spending too much time in the kitchen.

MIXED TOMATO SALAD

A simple, but colourful salad of different tomatoes, which will complement many summer flavours.

4 beef tomatoes, washed and thinly sliced

225 g/8 oz cherry tomatoes, halved

8 sun-dried tomatoes in oil, finely chopped

150 g/5 oz mozzarella cheese (omit for vegan*)

handful of fresh basil

few sprigs of fresh oregano

fresh edible flowers, to garnish

For the dressing:

2 tablespoons oil from the sun-dried tomatoes

2 teaspoons balsamic vinegar

1 tablespoon white wine vinegar

salt and freshly ground black pepper

■ Arrange the sliced beef tomato on a platter. Scatter the cherry tomato halves and sun-dried tomatoes over the top.

■ Cut the mozzarella into tiny chunks and scatter over the tomatoes (if using).

■ Mix the dressing ingredients together and drizzle over the tomatoes and cheese.

■ Use the basil and oregano leaves and edible flowers to decorate the salad.

ITALIAN SPINACH
AND RICOTTA GNOCCHI

It can be difficult to get a good vegetarian Parmesan and you will often find that a vegetarian Pecorino is a much tastier alternative.

200 g/7 oz baby spinach leaves
150 g/5 oz ricotta cheese
50 g/2 oz plain white flour
60 g/2½ oz vegetarian Pecorino or
   Parmesan, grated
1 free-range egg yolk
pinch of nutmeg
salt and freshly ground black pepper
extra Pecorino or Parmesan, grated

For the tomato sauce:
1 tablespoon olive oil

1 small red onion, finely chopped
1 small piece fennel or celery, finely
   chopped (optional)
1 garlic clove, crushed
450 g/1 lb fresh tomatoes, skinned,
   deseeded and chopped
150 ml/¼ pint white wine
4 sun-dried tomatoes in oil, chopped
2 tablespoons chopped fresh
   flat-leaf parsley
salt and freshly ground black
   pepper

■ First, make the tomato sauce. Heat the oil in a saucepan, add the onion, fennel or celery, if using, and the garlic and cook gently until tender. Add the fresh tomatoes and white wine and bring to the boil. Simmer for about 10 minutes, until starting to reduce and thicken. Stir in the sun-dried tomatoes, parsley and seasoning to taste. Keep warm.

■ Wash the spinach and cook for 1-2 minutes in a covered pan in just the water left clinging to the leaves. Turn into a sieve and press down well to remove as much liquid as possible. Chop the drained spinach.

■ Beat the spinach into the ricotta cheese, together with the flour, 60 g/2½ oz of the Pecorino or Parmesan and enough egg yolk to bind. Season well with nutmeg, salt and pepper.

■ Use floured hands to help you shape the mixture, about 1 teaspoon at a time, into little balls. Bring a large pan of water to the boil and drop batches of the gnocchi into the simmering water. Cook for 3-4 minutes, until they float on the surface. Remove with a slotted spoon and place in a greased ovenproof dish.

■ Pour the sauce over the gnocchi and sprinkle with some grated cheese. Place under a hot grill until the cheese has melted, then serve immediately.

Opposite: Italian spinach and ricotta gnocchi

**SUMMER
MENU 3**
▪
SERVES 4
▪

Stuffed baked
tomatoes with olives

Penne tossed with
artichokes and
mozzarella

Lemon mille feuilles
(see page 122)

**SUITABLE FOR
VEGANS**

STUFFED BAKED
TOMATOES WITH OLIVES

A very simple starter, these tomatoes can be served either hot or chilled, with some crusty bread.

4 tablespoons bulgar wheat
4 large tomatoes
1 tablespoon olive oil
1 small onion, finely chopped
1 garlic clove, crushed
50 g/2 oz oyster mushrooms, chopped
4 tablespoons sweetcorn kernels (canned or frozen)
4 sun-dried tomatoes in oil, chopped
8 kalamata olives, stoned and finely chopped
1 tablespoon chopped oregano or basil
salt and freshly ground black pepper
sprigs of parsley, to garnish

■ Preheat the oven to 190°C/375°F/Gas Mark 5.
■ Put the bulgar wheat in a bowl and pour boiling water over to cover. Leave to soak for 15–20 minutes, until tender. Drain off any excess water.
■ Cut the tops off the tomatoes and reserve. Scoop out the seeds and some of the flesh. Turn upside-down on kitchen paper to drain.
■ Heat the olive oil and fry the onion and garlic until tender. Add the oyster mushrooms and fry for 2 minutes. Stir in the sweetcorn, sun-dried tomatoes, olives, bulgar wheat and herbs and season well.
■ Pack the filling into the tomatoes and top each with a tomato 'lid'. Place in a greased ovenproof dish and bake in the preheated oven for 30–40 minutes. Serve either hot or cooled, garnished with parsley sprigs.

Serves 4

PENNE TOSSED WITH
ARTICHOKES AND MOZZARELLA

This dish is tasty with or without the mozzarella cheese. It is quick to cook so it doesn't involve staying in a hot kitchen for too long, making it ideal for summer entertaining.

225 g /8 oz penne pasta
400-g /14-oz can of artichoke hearts
3 tablespoons olive oil
400-g /14-oz can of chopped tomatoes
12 black olives, stoned and roughly chopped
2 tablespoons vegan pesto
salt and freshly ground black pepper
150 g /5 oz mozzarella cheese, sliced (omit for vegans*)
few sprigs of fresh basil, to garnish

■ Cook the pasta as instructed on the packet until tender but still firm (*al dente*). Drain well.

■ Meanwhile, drain and quarter the artichoke hearts, place on a grill pan and drizzle with 2 tablespoons of olive oil. Grill, turning occasionally, until golden.

■ Heat the remaining olive oil in a saucepan, add the chopped tomatoes, black olives and pesto and cook for 2 minutes. Stir in the grilled artichokes and season to taste with salt and pepper.

■ Toss in the cooked pasta, turn into an ovenproof dish and top with mozzarella, if using. Place under a hot grill until the mozzarella has melted. Garnish with fresh basil leaves and serve with a salad.

DRINKS TIP
■

For those of you wanting non-alcoholic drinks, some elderflower cordial mixed to taste with soda water is wonderfully refreshing on a hot sunny day.

WINE SUGGESTIONS
■

White
Volcanic Hills Harslevelu
Deep flavoured Hungarian with a hint of spice

Red
Chianti San Vito
Medium bodied, fresh and well rounded

CHRISTMAS
AND WINTER ENTERTAINING

Left: Chocolate, brandy and hazelnut yule log (page 58), and Mushroom stuffed filo parcels (page 54)

*CAN BE VEGAN

PEAR, CELERIAC
AND STILTON SOUP

Celeriac always seems to be the poor relation of the root vegetables as people tend to look at its knobbly exterior and shy away from experimenting with it. This is a pity as it has a slightly sweet celery flavour and purées to a beautifully smooth texture. If you cannot obtain celeriac, then try using a squash instead.

675 g / 1½ lb pears, peeled and cored
2 tablespoons sunflower oil
1 onion, chopped
450 g / 1 lb celeriac, peeled and roughly chopped
1.2 litres/2 pints vegetable stock
salt and freshly ground black pepper
175-225 g /6-8 oz vegetarian Stilton cheese, crumbled (omit for vegans*)
single cream or soya cream*, to serve
chopped chives, to garnish

■ Cut the pears into slices and poach them in 300 ml/½ pint water until they are tender. Blend the pears and water together and reserve.
■ Heat the oil in a large saucepan and gently fry the onion until translucent.
■ Add the celeriac and cook, covered, for 10-15 minutes, or until tender.
■ Add the vegetable stock and blended pears, bring to the boil and then reduce the heat and simmer for 10 minutes.
■ Liquidize the soup in a blender or food processor and return to a clean pan. Reheat gently, season to taste and stir in the crumbled Stilton*, if using.
■ Serve immediately with a swirl of dairy or soya cream* and a sprinkling of chopped chives.

FESTIVE CHESTNUT
BREAD ROLLS

*CAN BE VEGAN

These rolls complement the fruit flavours in the Pear, Celeriac and Stilton Soup (opposite), and the Apple, Mushroom and Calvados Soup (see page 59). They are also delicious with cheese.

175 g/6 oz strong wholemeal flour
175 g/6 oz strong white flour
$^{1}/_{2}$ teaspoon salt
$^{1}/_{2}$ teaspoon ground nutmeg or cinnamon
12 g/$^{1}/_{2}$ oz fresh yeast (or 1 teaspoon dried yeast)
2 teaspoons sugar
240 ml/8 fl oz (approx.) hand-hot water
100 g/4 oz chestnuts (cooked weight), chopped
dairy or soya milk*, to glaze

■ Preheat the oven to 220°C/425°F/Gas Mark 7.
■ Mix the flours, salt and the nutmeg or cinnamon together in a large mixing bowl. Cream the yeast and sugar together and add a little hand-hot water. Mix well and leave in a warm place for 5 minutes, until frothy.
■ Pour the yeast mixture over the flour in the bowl and add enough water, one tablespoon at a time, to make a stiff, but not sticky, dough.
■ Tip the dough out onto a floured work surface and knead for 10 minutes. Place the dough in a clean, lightly oiled bowl, cover with a clean tea towel or loose cling film and leave in a warm place until doubled in size (about 1 hour).
■ Punch the dough down, turn out onto a floured surface, add the chopped chestnuts and knead for 5 minutes, making sure that the chestnuts are evenly distributed throughout the mixture.
■ Divide into 6 balls and shape into rolls. Allow to prove by leaving the rolls in a warm place for 20-30 minutes, until well risen. Glaze with dairy or soya milk* and bake for 15-20 minutes in the preheated oven. If the the rolls sound hollow when tapped on the base, then they are cooked.

Makes 6 rolls

*CAN BE VEGAN

MUSHROOM STUFFED
FILO PARCELS

TIP

■

A tasty alternative filling is
to top the mushrooms
with a piece of vegetarian
Brie in place of the
stuffing, and then top this
with the cranberry or
redcurrant sauce. In the
summer, you could fill
each mushroom with
ricotta and spinach and
top with a teaspoon of
peach chutney to give a
Mediterranean flavour to
the parcels.

Use your favourite vegetarian stuffing mix in this recipe or make your own. This recipe is excellent for Christmas in a family that has only one or two vegetarian members or is perhaps entertaining a vegetarian guest. The parcels can be assembled and then refrigerated for 24 hours before cooking them and completing the dish. Indeed, most of the ingredients will be part of everyone's Christmas meal.

6 medium-sized field mushrooms (flat)
oil to fry the mushrooms
225 g/8 oz packet fresh or frozen
    filo pastry
25 g/1 oz butter or vegan
    margarine*, melted
6 teaspoons cranberry or
    redcurrant sauce
extra cranberry or redcurrant
    sauce, to serve

Hazelnut stuffing:
1 packet vegetarian stuffing mix,
    e.g. parsley, lemon and thyme
1 small onion, finely chopped
1 stick celery, finely chopped
15 g/½ oz butter or vegan
    margarine*
25-50 g/1-2 oz roasted hazelnuts,
    chopped
milk, dairy or soya*, for binding

■ Preheat the oven to 190°C/375°F/Gas Mark 5.
■ Fry the mushrooms for 3-4 minutes on each side until tender, then cool. Make up the stuffing mix of your choice. Fry the onion and celery in the butter or margarine*, and then add the stuffing mix and hazelnuts. Add a little milk (dairy or soya*) if necessary to bind together. Leave to cool.
■ Fill each flat field mushroom with the stuffing mixture.
■ Take 3 sheets of filo pastry at a time. Cut them in half so that you have 10–12.5-cm/4–5-in squares. Take one square and brush with a little melted butter or margarine. Place another square on top at an angle, and brush again. Do the same with a third sheet.
■ Place a stuffed mushroom in the middle of the filo pastry, and top with a teaspoon of cranberry or redcurrant sauce. Bring the edges of the pastry up together and pinch them to form a little parcel (money-bag shape). Make up the rest of the parcels in the same way.
■ Brush with melted butter or margarine* and place on a greased baking tray. Bake in the preheated oven for 15-20 minutes, until the pastry is crisp and golden. Serve hot with extra cranberry or redcurrant sauce.

ORANGE CARROTS
AND SWEET POTATOES

*CAN BE VEGAN

As Christmas is a special occasion, it's always a good idea to use some slightly more exotic or unusual vegetables to accompany the festive dinner. This dish makes a delicious change from the traditional brussels sprouts and roasted parsnips.

450 g / 1 lb sweet potatoes, peeled
15 g / ½ oz butter or vegan margarine*
175 ml / 6 fl oz orange juice
2.5-cm / 1-in piece of root ginger, peeled, grated and juice squeezed out
grated zest of ½ orange
450 g / 1 lb carrots, peeled and cut into matchsticks
salt and freshly ground black pepper
chopped parsley, to garnish

■ Parboil the sweet potatoes in boiling lightly salted water for 10 minutes, then drain and cut into cubes.
■ Melt the butter or margarine* in a saucepan. Add the orange juice, ginger juice, orange zest, sweet potatoes and carrots. Bring to the boil. Reduce the heat, cover the pan and simmer for 8-10 minutes, until the vegetables are tender.
■ Remove the pan lid, turn up the heat and boil the liquid in the pan until syrupy, stirring frequently. Season to taste with salt and freshly ground black pepper.
■ Transfer the glazed vegetables to a warm serving dish and sprinkle with chopped parsley.

Below: Mushroom stuffed filo parcels

SUITABLE FOR
VEGANS

ROAST POTATOES
AND PARSNIPS

By parboiling the potatoes and then roughening the flat side with a fork, they become very crispy when roasted, whereas the onion rings become slightly charred.

6 medium potatoes, peeled and halved lengthways
4 parsnips, peeled and sliced
good pinch of dried mixed herbs
2 onions, cut into thin rings
4–6 tablespoons sunflower or olive oil
salt and freshly ground black pepper
225 g/8 oz cherry tomatoes

■ Preheat the oven to 200°C/400°F/Gas Mark 6.
■ Parboil the potatoes for 10 minutes until the outsides are slightly soft. Drain and place in a roasting tin flat side up. Use a fork to roughen the flat uppermost side of the potato.
■ Add the prepared parsnips, sprinkle with mixed herbs and arrange the onion rings over the top. Drizzle with sunflower or olive oil and season with salt and lots of black pepper.
■ Roast for 40 minutes, basting several times, then add the cherry tomatoes and bake for a further 15–20 minutes, until all the vegetables are cooked and the tomatoes have split open.
■ Serve the roast vegetables with steamed broccoli, brussels sprouts or mange tout with your Christmas meal.

**WINE
SUGGESTIONS**
■

White
Estate Chardonnay,
Millton Estate
*Rich and ripe New
Zealand dry white*

Red
Valréas Côtes du
Rhône Villages
*Award winning spicy red
with great structure*

BREAD SAUCE
WITH ROASTED GARLIC

Adding creamed roasted garlic to this traditional accompaniment to Christmas dinner lifts it out of the ordinary. Your guests will be trying to guess the mystery ingredient.

TIP

■

This sauce can be made in advance and frozen until required.

1 head of garlic
3 tablespoons olive oil
6 cloves
1 onion, peeled and left whole
1 bay leaf
6 whole peppercorns
300 ml/½ pint milk (dairy or soya*)
50 g/2 oz fresh white breadcrumbs
15 g/½ oz butter or vegan margarine*
salt and freshly ground black pepper
grated nutmeg
2 tablespoons cream (omit for vegan*)

■ Preheat the oven to 200°C/400°F/Gas Mark 6.

■ Break the garlic into cloves, leaving the skin on. Place in a small ovenproof dish, drizzle with olive oil and bake in the oven for 15–20 minutes, until tender when pierced with a knife. Remove from the oven and leave to cool.

■ Stick the cloves into the onion and place in a saucepan with the bay leaf, peppercorns and milk (dairy or soya*). Bring to the boil, then take the pan off the heat and add the breadcrumbs. Stir in the butter or margarine* and leave to stand for 30 minutes.

■ Squeeze the garlic out of their skins and mash until you have a creamy textured purée.

■ Remove the peppercorns, onion and bay leaf from the sauce, and stir in the creamed garlic. Season to taste with salt, pepper and nutmeg and stir in the cream (omit for vegan*), if using. Reheat gently to serve.

CHOCOLATE, BRANDY
AND HAZELNUT YULE LOG

If the thought of rolling a roulade is too complicated for you, leave the sponge to cool, trim the edges and cut into three pieces. Divide the brandy cream and cherries into four and layer up the sponge with cream and cherries in between. Top with cream and use the last portion to pipe rosettes around the edge. Decorate with cherry halves and grated chocolate.

For the roulade:
175 g/6 oz plain chocolate
2 tablespoons brandy
5 free-range eggs, separated
175 g/6 oz caster sugar
100 g/4 oz hazelnuts, roasted
icing sugar, for dusting

For the filling:
1-2 tablespoons brandy
300 ml/½ pint double cream, whipped
425-g/15-oz can of black cherries,
    drained, stoned and halved
icing sugar, for dusting
sprig of holly

■ Preheat the oven to 190°C/375°F/Gas Mark 5. Line a 33 x 23-cm/13 x 9-in Swiss roll tin with non-stick baking parchment.
■ Melt the chocolate in a bowl over a saucepan of simmering water. Stir in the brandy and leave to cool a little.
■ Whisk the egg yolks and sugar in a large bowl, again over a pan of simmering water, until the mixture becomes thick and creamy.
■ Combine the cooled chocolate and egg yolk mixture. Grind the hazelnuts and fold in the chocolate mixture.
■ In a grease-free bowl, whisk the egg whites until stiff. Fold into the chocolate mixture with a metal spoon until no whites can be seen.
■ Pour into the prepared Swiss roll tin and spread evenly. Cook in the preheated oven for 20-25 minutes, until the sponge springs back when lightly pressed.
■ Lay a sheet of baking parchment on a wire cooling tray and turn the roulade out onto it. Cover with a clean damp tea towel before peeling off the lining parchment. Trim the edges.
■ Transfer the roulade and parchment to the work top. Roll up the roulade with the parchment inside and leave to rest for 5 minutes.
■ Fold the brandy into the cream. Unroll the roulade and spread the cream over the surface, leaving a 1.5-cm/½-in gap along one long edge. Scatter with the cherries and roll up. Dust with icing sugar and decorate with holly.

Serves 6–8

APPLE, MUSHROOM
AND CALVADOS SOUP

Calvados, the apple brandy from Normandy, gives a boost to the slightly sweet and fruity flavour of this unusual soup. Ordinary brandy can be substituted if preferred.

2 tablespoons groundnut oil
225 g / 8 oz onions, finely chopped
225 g / 8 oz potatoes, finely chopped
225 g / 8 oz mushrooms, chopped
600 ml / 1 pint vegetable stock
300 ml / ½ pint apple juice
salt and freshly ground black pepper
4–6 tablespoons Calvados (or brandy)
single cream or soya cream* to serve

■ Heat the oil in a saucepan and fry the onions until starting to brown. Add the potatoes and mushrooms and cook gently for 5 minutes.
■ Add the stock and apple juice, bring to the boil and simmer for 20-30 minutes. Allow to cool and then blend until smooth in a blender or food processor.
■ Return the puréed soup to a clean pan and gently reheat. Season and stir in the Calvados. Serve garnished with a swirl of cream.

WINTER MENU 1

•

SERVES 4

•

Apple, mushroom and Calvados soup

Griddled aubergine stacks

Exotic fruit tatin with butterscotch sauce

*CAN BE VEGAN

GRIDDLED
AUBERGINE STACKS

**WINE
SUGGESTIONS**
■

White
Volcanic Hills
Sauvignon Blanc
Full fruited, crisp dry wine

Red
Château la Blanquerie
Bordeaux Supérieur
*Classically clean and well
poised claret*

This recipe is completely dairy free, but if you like cheese these vegetable stacks are lovely topped with a slice of griddled Halloumi. The sauce should be dotted with lots of tiny pieces of tomato and pepper, which form the 'confetti'.

a little olive oil
1 large aubergine, cut into rings
2 beef tomatoes, skinned and cut
    into rings
zest of 1 lemon, finely chopped
few sprigs of fresh sage, chopped
few sprigs of fresh thyme, chopped
few fresh chives, finely chopped
salt and freshly ground black pepper
balsamic vinegar, to taste
4 slices Halloumi cheese
lemon zest, to garnish
chives or chive flowers, to garnish

Tomato confetti sauce:
1 tablespoon olive oil
1 small onion, finely chopped
1 garlic clove, crushed
225 g/8 oz fresh ripe full-flavoured
    tomatoes, skinned and finely
    chopped
150 ml/¼ pint vegetarian white wine
1 yellow or red pepper, roasted, skin
    removed and cut into strips, then
    across into diamonds
1 teaspoon balsamic vinegar
salt and pepper

■ First, make the sauce. Heat the olive oil in a saucepan and fry the onion gently with the garlic. Add half of the chopped tomatoes and the white wine and cook for 5 minutes. Blend until smooth. Mix in the rest of the chopped tomatoes with the pepper pieces and 1 teaspoon of balsamic vinegar. Season to taste.

■ Brush the griddle with olive oil and cook the aubergine slices so that they are seared with stripes. Put on one side and keep warm. Grill the beef tomato slices gently.

■ Mix the lemon and herbs together and season well. On individual serving plates, layer the aubergine, tomato and herb mix. Drizzle with a little balsamic vinegar. Repeat until all the layers are used up and top with a slice of tomato and a sprinkling of the herb mixture. Grill the slices of Halloumi and arrange on top of each stack, garnished with lemon zest and chives. Drizzle tomato confetti sauce around the plate and decorate with chives or chive flowers. Serve warm.

Opposite: Griddled aubergine stacks

*CAN BE VEGAN

EXOTIC FRUIT TATIN
WITH BUTTERSCOTCH SAUCE

TIP

■

The pastry crust can be made very quickly in a food processor. Add just enough water to the rest of the ingredients to form a ball which comes away from the sides of the processor bowl. Then rest in the refrigerator and continue as before.

Use a solid-based cake tin. The juices will leak out of a loose-based tin.

The original Tatin or 'upside down tart' was made with apples, but you can vary the fruits or even make a savoury version (see page 39). By cooking the pastry on top of the fruit and then turning it out so that the pastry becomes the base you achieve a crisp rather than a soggy crust with the fruit in a thick syrup. Add the rich butterscotch sauce for anyone with a really sweet tooth and/or dairy or soya cream to complete this dessert.

50 g/2 oz butter or vegan
  margarine*
225 g/8 oz fresh pineapple,
  sliced
1 ripe mango, sliced
1 banana, cut into rings
2–3 tablespoons dark muscovado
  sugar
1 tablespoon rum
partially opened physalis (optional)
icing sugar, for dusting
dairy cream or soya cream*

Pastry crust:
100 g/4 oz plain white flour
pinch of cinnamon or mixed spice
50 g/2 oz butter or vegan margarine*
7–8 tablespoons iced water

**Butterscotch sauce
(not vegan):**
75 g/3 oz butter
200 g/7 oz dark muscovado sugar
2 tablespoons golden syrup
75 ml/3 fl oz double cream

■ Preheat the oven to 200°C/400°F/Gas Mark 6.

■ Make the pastry: sift the flour and spice into a bowl. Cut the butter or margarine* into small pieces, then rub in with the fingertips to a breadcrumb consistency. Add sufficient water to mix to a dough. Roll into a ball, wrap in cling film and refrigerate for 30 minutes.

■ For the topping: melt the butter or margarine* in a frying pan and gently fry all the fruit until just tender. Stir in the sugar until melted. Take off the heat, stir in the rum and leave to cool. Place the fruit mixture in a 21-cm/8½-in round non-stick, solid-based shallow cake tin.

■ Roll out the pastry crust dough, cover the fruit and trim the edges to fit. Bake in the preheated oven for about 20 minutes, until golden.

■ Turn out by inverting the tatin onto a serving plate. Decorate with physalis and icing sugar and serve with butterscotch sauce, cream or soya cream*.

■ To make the butterscotch sauce, melt the butter, sugar and syrup in a small pan over a gentle heat, stirring all the time. Stir in the cream and serve.

WARM AVOCADO
SALAD WITH RED PEPPER DRESSING

WINTER MENU 2
∎
SERVES 4
∎

Warm avocado salad with red pepper dressing

Rosti stacks with spicy peach coulis

Warm puy lentil salad

Red cabbage and onion salad

Panettone bread and butter pudding

SUITABLE FOR VEGANS

Avocados are usually served cold, but frying them quickly develops the flavour and adds a new dimension. You could also drizzle a mixture of olive oil, raspberry vinegar and a dash of balsamic vinegar over the top for a summery variation to this dish.

1 red pepper
2 garlic cloves, left whole with skins intact
olive oil, to drizzle
50 g/2 oz ground almonds
5 tablespoons extra virgin olive oil
1 tablespoon Dijon mustard
1 tablespoon balsamic vinegar
1 tablespoon chopped fresh coriander
150 ml/1/4 pint dry white wine
salt and freshly ground black pepper
2 large ripe avocados, peeled and stoned
1 packet mixed salad leaves
fresh coriander, to garnish

∎ Preheat the oven to 200°C/400°F/Gas Mark 6.
∎ Place the red pepper and whole cloves of garlic on a baking sheet and drizzle with olive oil. Roast until the pepper skin is starting to blacken and char and the garlic is soft when pierced with a knife. Remove the skin and seeds from the pepper, retaining the juices, and squeeze the garlic out of the skins.
∎ Blend the red pepper flesh, reserved juice, garlic, ground almonds, 3 tablespoons of the olive oil, mustard, vinegar and coriander together until smooth.
∎ Add the wine and blend until the desired consistency is reached. Season to taste, pour into a saucepan and set aside.
∎ Cut the avocados in half and then into slices. Heat the remaining olive oil in a non-stick frying pan and, when hot, quickly toss the avocados in the oil until heated through but not soft.
∎ Heat the sauce gently over low heat. Meanwhile, arrange the mixed salad leaves on 4 serving plates with the avocado slices on top. Drizzle the warm sauce over them and serve garnished with fresh coriander leaves.

ROSTI STACKS
WITH SPICY PEACH COULIS

Although there are several elements to this dish, it is relatively easy to prepare and each stage can be made in advance and then refrigerated. The spicy peach coulis is an unusual contrasting taste.

2 large potatoes
350 g/12 oz celeriac or parsnips
pinch of ground nutmeg
salt and freshly ground black pepper
3 tablespoons olive oil
2 onions, sliced
1 tablespoon soft brown sugar
225 g/8 oz mushrooms, sliced
1 garlic clove, crushed
fresh parsley and basil leaves, to
  garnish

Gremolata:
50 g/2 oz vegan margarine, softened

1 garlic clove, crushed
juice and zest of 1/2 lemon
few sprigs of fresh parsley, chopped
few sprigs of fresh basil, chopped
salt and freshly ground black
  pepper

Spicy peach coulis:
2 small onions, very finely chopped
1 tablespoon olive oil
1–2 tablespoons mild curry
  powder
225 g/8 oz peach chutney
4–5 tablespoons water

■ Preheat the oven to 200°C/400°F/Gas Mark 6.
■ Peel the potatoes and celeriac or parsnips. Halve the potatoes and cut the celeriac into similar-sized pieces. Par-boil for 5 minutes (if using parsnips, leave raw), then drain and coarsely grate. Season with the nutmeg, salt and pepper.
■ Grease a baking sheet and arrange the mixed grated vegetables in four 10-cm/4-in mounds. Flatten with a spatula and make a depression in the centre, drizzle with a little olive oil, then bake for 25-30 minutes, until golden.
■ Meanwhile, fry the onions in 1 tablespoon olive oil until golden brown, then stir in the sugar and seasoning. Remove from the heat and keep warm. Cook the mushrooms and garlic in the remaining olive oil for 5 minutes. Season and keep warm.
■ Make the gremolata by beating all the ingredients until well blended.
■ Take the rostis out of the oven. Top with the onions, then the mushrooms and finally the gremolata. Return to the oven for 10 minutes to heat through.
■ Meanwhile, make the coulis. Gently fry the onions in the oil until tender, add the curry powder and cook for 2 minutes, stirring all the time. Add the chutney and water and heat through gently. Blend until smooth.
■ Place the rostis on serving plates and pour a little coulis around each one. Garnish with fresh parsley and basil.

Opposite: Rosti stacks with spicy peach coulis

WINTER SALADS

WARM PUY LENTIL SALAD

100 g/4 oz puy lentils (dry
  weight), cooked
1 bunch spring onions, chopped
6 radishes, halved and sliced
1 orange, segmented
chicory and radicchio leaves to
  serve
1 free-range egg, hard-boiled and
  finely chopped, to serve
  (omit for vegans*)

For the dressing:
1 tablespoon rosemary, finely
  chopped
1 teaspoon Dijon mustard
2 tablespoons red wine vinegar
1 tablespoon orange juice
3 tablespoons extra virgin olive oil
zest of ½ orange, finely chopped
pinch of sugar
salt and pepper, to taste

■ Cook the lentils and keep warm. Prepare the spring onions, radishes
and orange and mix into the lentils.
■ Make the dressing and pour over the warm lentils.
■ Arrange the chicory and radicchio leaves around the edge of a serving
platter. Pile the lentils in the centre and sprinkle the finely chopped hard-
boiled egg (omit for vegans*) over the top. Serve immediately.

RED CABBAGE AND ONION SALAD

3 tablespoons olive oil
1 teaspoon cumin seeds
100 g/4 oz red cabbage, shredded
1 red onion, halved and finely sliced
25–50 g/1–2 oz sultanas or
  raisins, soaked and drained

1 tablespoon cider vinegar
salt and ground black pepper
1 head Chinese leaves, finely
  shredded
6 spring onions, topped and tailed
1 garlic clove, crushed

■ Heat 2 tablespoons of the olive oil in a frying pan and add the cumin
seeds, stirring for a few minutes until they start to colour and pop. Add
the red cabbage and stir-fry for 5 minutes. Remove from the heat and
add the red onion, sultanas or raisins and cider vinegar. Season to taste.
■ Arrange the shredded Chinese leaves around the edge of a platter.
Put the red cabbage in the centre.
■ Heat the remaining olive oil and quickly fry the spring onions and
garlic. Arrange on top of the cabbage and serve.

*CAN BE VEGAN

TIP
■
Pick the lentils over very
carefully before soaking
and cooking as they often
contain small pieces of grit.

**SUITABLE FOR
VEGANS**

TIP
■
If the spring onions
are large, cut into
1-cm/½-inch pieces on
a slant before cooking,
then scatter over the
red cabbage.

PANETTONE BREAD
AND BUTTER PUDDING

I have never found a vegetarian panettone in the shops, so make my own and use the day-old bread for this recipe. If you prefer not to make your own, this recipe works just as well with any fruit and nut bread. Add extra sultanas to increase the fruity flavour.

1 panettone or other fruit and nut bread, sliced
50 g / 2 oz butter
3 free-range eggs
50 g / 2 oz caster sugar
2 tablespoons rum or brandy
few drops of vanilla essence
300 ml / 1/2 pint milk
300 ml / 1/2 pint double cream
1 tablespoon demerara sugar
1 teaspoon ground nutmeg

■ Preheat the oven to 180°C/350°F/Gas Mark 4.
■ Grease a shallow ovenproof baking dish. Remove the crusts from the panettone slices. Butter the panettone and arrange the slices in the prepared dish, overlapping each other.
■ Beat together the eggs, caster sugar, rum or brandy and vanilla essence.
■ Heat the milk and cream gently in a saucepan, then bring to the boil. Remove from the heat immediately and pour onto the egg and sugar mixture, stirring all the time.
■ Pour the mixture over the panettone. Mix the demerara sugar and nutmeg together and sprinkle over the top.
■ Stand the dish in a bain-marie (a baking dish half-filled with water) and bake in the preheated oven for 45-50 minutes, until the custard is set and the top is golden.

TIP
■

Bread and butter pudding is a basic but very adaptable dish. Try spreading plain or fruit bread with jam or marmalade before arranging the slices in the dish; or vary the spices and alcohol used, to change the flavours.

**WINTER
MENU 3**
■
SERVES 4
■

Chestnut and red
wine pâté

Gougère of
caramelized
vegetables

Roast vegetable
purées

Gomasio potatoes

Mango, pineapple
and orange fool

**SUITABLE FOR
VEGANS**

CHESTNUT
AND RED WINE PATE

This is a very simple but rich and tasty recipe, which is useful as a sandwich filling as well as a dinner party starter. Buy canned, ready-cooked chestnuts and chestnut purée to make it even easier.

1 tablespoon olive or groundnut oil
1 small onion, finely chopped
1 garlic clove, crushed
pinch of dried thyme
150 ml/¼ pint red wine
150 ml/¼ pint vegetable stock
100 g/4 oz chopped chestnuts
   (cooked weight)
100 g/4 oz chestnut purée

75 g/3 oz wholemeal breadcrumbs
1 tablespoon brandy
2–3 teaspoons shoyu
salt and freshly ground black pepper

To serve:
fresh herbs
crackers
crisp green salad leaves

■ Heat the oil in a saucepan, and gently cook the onion and garlic with the dried thyme until soft. Add the red wine and vegetable stock and bring to the boil.

■ Remove from the heat and stir in the chopped chestnuts, chestnut purée, breadcrumbs, brandy and shoyu. Season with salt and pepper to taste. Cook over a gentle heat until thickened.

■ Spoon the pâté into individual ramekins, smooth the surface and then chill in the refrigerator until required.

■ Serve garnished with fresh herbs, with crackers and crisp green salad leaves.

GOUGERE OF
CARAMELIZED VEGETABLES

Agougère is simply a ring of choux pastry 'buns'. Other ingredients can be used to fill the centre of the ring. The caramelized root vegetables in this recipe are wonderfully sweet.

4 tablespoons olive oil

6 garlic cloves, peeled and left whole

8 shallots, halved

3 medium carrots, cut into matchsticks

3 medium parsnips, cut into matchsticks

225 g/8 oz sweet potatoes or butternut squash, cut into 1-cm/½-in cubes

pinch of dried basil (or other herb)

1 tablespoon sugar or apple juice concentrate

225 ml/8 fl oz vegetable stock

2 teaspoons tomato purée

salt and freshly ground black pepper

torn fresh basil leaves, to garnish

Choux pastry:

100 g/4 oz plain white flour

pinch of salt

pinch of dried basil (or other herb)

200 ml/7 fl oz water

75 g/3 oz butter

3 free range eggs, lightly beaten

75 g/3 oz vegetarian Cheddar cheese, grated

WINE SUGGESTIONS

■

White

Opou Riesling
Millton Vineyard
*Light, honeyed and
medium-dry kiwi white*

Red

Domaine St Michel
Syrah/Malbec
*Tasty Midi red with good
up-front fruit*

■ Preheat the oven to 220°C/425°F/Gas Mark 7.

■ Sauté the garlic, shallots and carrots in the oil for 5 minutes, until lightly browned. Add the parsnips, sweet potato or squash and dried basil, and sauté for 5 minutes.

■ Add the sugar or apple juice concentrate and stir well. Add the stock and tomato purée, bring to the boil, then reduce the heat and simmer gently until the vegetables are tender. Season and set aside, keeping warm.

■ For the choux pastry, line a greased baking sheet with baking parchment. Mix the flour, salt and dried basil together in a jug. Heat the water and butter gently in a medium-sized saucepan until the butter has melted, and then bring to the boil. Remove from the heat and pour in all the flour at once and beat thoroughly with a wooden spoon. Continue beating over a gentle heat until the flour is incorporated and you have a ball of pastry in the pan.

■ Remove from the heat, cool for 2 minutes, then beat in the eggs, a little at a time. Fold in the cheese and beat well. Spoon the mixture onto the lined baking tray, one tablespoon at a time, to form a ring.

■ Bake in the preheated oven for 20 minutes, until risen and golden. Reduce the temperature to 180°C/350°F/Gas Mark 4 and make small slits in the side of each 'bun' to allow steam to escape. Bake for a further 5 minutes.

■ Transfer the gougère to a serving dish. Reheat the filling and spoon into the centre of the ring. Serve garnished with torn basil leaves.

WINTER
VEGETABLE DISHES

ROAST VEGETABLE PURÉES

Seasonal winter root vegetables are naturally sweet in flavour. As an alternative to mashed potatoes, try making a vegetable purée. Some delicious combinations are:

- Celeriac and ground cumin
- Carrot and ground (or fresh) coriander
- Sweet potato or butternut squash with nutmeg
- Potatoes with saffron and garlic

Boil the vegetable used in the usual way until very tender. Mash with butter or vegan margarine* to taste, then add enough milk or cream (or soya milk* or soya cream*) to give a creamy texture. Add the suggested seasoning and use a piping bag with a large nozzle to pipe a 'nest' or a swirl of the purée on each serving plate, if liked.

GOMASIO POTATOES

The gomasio coating gives the potatoes a distinctive savoury flavour. Just split the cooked potatoes and fill with butter or vegan margarine* to serve.

4 medium-sized baking potatoes
olive oil to coat

For the gomasio:
5 teaspoons sesame seeds
½–1 teaspoon sea salt

- Preheat the oven to 200°C/400°F/Gas Mark 6.
- Scrub the baking potatoes and prick them with a fork. Rub the skins with a little olive oil.
- Dry toast the sesame seeds in a non-stick frying pan until they begin to pop. Put into a grinder with the sea salt and grind until smooth.
- Transfer to a plate and roll the potatoes in the gomasio to coat. Place on a baking tray and cook in the preheated oven for 45–60 minutes, until tender.

MANGO, PINEAPPLE
AND ORANGE FOOL

Exotic fruits are available in the supermarkets all the year round. They brighten up the usual wintry fare of apples, pears and oranges, whereas in the summer they add even more colour to the locally grown soft fruits. Although rich, this dessert is quite light and your guests are bound to come back for more, so there is enough for six helpings!

100 g / 4 oz vegetarian trifle sponges
   (or day-old sponge cake)
100 g / 4 oz canned pineapple slices
   in fruit juice
1 ripe mango, peeled, stoned and
   sliced (or use canned)
grated rind and juice of 2 oranges
25 g / 1 oz sugar

300 ml / 10 fl oz double cream
1-2 tablespoons Cointreau
   (optional)

To decorate:
curls of zest and segments of
   2 oranges
sprigs of fresh mint

■ Use the trifle sponges to line the base and halfway up the sides of a glass serving bowl. Drain the pineapple, reserving the juice, and arrange the slices of pineapple and mango over the sponges.

■ Pour 3 tablespoons of the reserved juice over the sponge to moisten. Mix the orange zest and juice with the sugar and stir until completely dissolved.

■ Whip the cream until thick, and then beat in the orange juice and sugar mixture, and the Cointreau, if using.

■ Pour over the fruit and sponge, then cover and chill in the refrigerator for at least 2 hours, until the juices have soaked into the sponge and the cream has thickened.

■ Just before serving, decorate the trifle with orange segments, curls of orange zest and sprigs of mint.

TIP
■
When choosing a mango, check that it is ripe by squeezing it gently in the palm of your hand — it should give slightly. Cut it in half lengthways, feeling down the side of the flat stone with your knife. Once the stone has been removed it can be skinned and sliced quite easily.

PARTY
CANAPES AND FINGER FOOD

Left: Party dips with mixed crudités (page 74), Asparagus and cashew mini tartlets (page 80) and Watermelon and strawberry punch (page 85)

SUITABLE FOR VEGANS

TIP
■

Ready-made vegan mayonnaise is now available from health food stores. Plain, or flavoured with lemon or garlic, it can be used as the basis of many different dips.

PARTY DIPS
WITH MIXED CRUDITÉS

This is a versatile vegan mayonnaise which can be flavoured with garlic and lemon to make a basic dip, or other ingredients can be added to change the flavour. You could also use the satay sauce from the mushroom satay recipe on page 93 as a party dip.

90 ml / 3 fl oz soya milk
juice and zest of ½ lemon
1 garlic clove, crushed
180 ml / 6 fl oz cold pressed
    sunflower oil
salt and freshly ground black pepper

Mexican dip:
1 tablespoon chopped coriander
½ avocado, finely chopped
1 tomato, skinned and finely chopped

Curry dip:
1 small onion or shallot
1 tablespoon groundnut oil

1 tablespoon mild curry powder
    or paste
2 tablespoons spicy mango chutney

For the crudités and dippers:
1 red pepper, deseeded and sliced
1 green pepper, deseeded and sliced
1 yellow pepper, deseeded and sliced
3 sticks celery, cut into 5-cm/2-in
    lengths
½ cucumber, cut into thick
    matchsticks
2 carrots, cut into batons
3 pitta breads, cut into triangles
1 packet vegetarian tortilla chips

■ For each dip, you need one quantity of the basic dip recipe. Place the soya milk, lemon juice and zest and garlic in a blender and blend together briefly. Gradually drizzle in the oil through the feed tube with the motor running until the mixture emulsifies. Season to taste.

■ If wished, add one of the suggested flavourings. For the Mexican dip, the chopped coriander, avocado and tomato can just be stirred in.

■ For the curry dip, fry the onion or shallot gently in the oil for 5 minutes, until tender. Add the curry powder or paste and cook for 2 minutes. Stir in the mango chutney. Remove from the heat and cool before stirring into the basic dip.

■ Serve the dips with a selection of the suggested crudités and dippers.

Each dip serves 6–8

PARTY FOOD TIPS

■ Party food needs to be easy to eat while standing, balancing a plate and a drink in an often crowded room. Finger or fork food is simplest, but try to avoid too many pastry-based dishes. Other useful edible bases are croustades, crostini or vegetable 'boats'.

■ Choose recipes that can be prepared in advance to allow you to enjoy the party too.

■ A selection of hot and cold dishes is good for winter parties. For food that is to be served warm, prepare in advance and reheat in batches.

■ In the summer, lots of dips and crunchy vegetable crudités for dippers are popular.

■ Have a selection of drinks available — red and white wine, beer or lager, perhaps an appropriate punch and some interesting non-alcoholic drinks for those who are driving or prefer to avoid alcohol. If making a punch, make it fruity and not too alcoholic.

■ Many supermarkets and off licences will loan glasses free if you buy your drinks from them; and some will let you have drinks on a sale or return basis — it is better to over- rather than underestimate.

■ Have a plentiful supply of napkins available in case of spills.

■ Make the buffet table as colourful as possible, perhaps following a particular theme. This helps to make the food look even more tempting.

■ Fill gaps on the table with (vegetarian) crisps and snacks.

Below: Mexican dip (see opposite)

OLIVE AND SUN-DRIED
TOMATO PALMIERS

When cold, the palmiers can be stored in an airtight container for 24 hours, then reheated to crisp them up just before serving.

25 g/1 oz strong Vegetarian Cheddar cheese, finely grated
25 g/1 oz vegetarian Stilton cheese, finely grated
25 g/1 oz vegetarian Parmesan or Pecorino, finely grated
225 g/8 oz puff pastry (fresh or frozen)
freshly ground black pepper
25 g/1 oz black olives, stoned and finely chopped
25 g/1 oz sun-dried tomatoes, finely chopped

■ Preheat the oven to 220°C/425°F/Gas Mark 7. Mix all the grated cheeses together in a bowl.

■ Roll out the pastry to an oblong strip, 30 x 20 cm/12 x 8 in. Sprinkle the cheese on two-thirds of the pastry, and sprinkle black pepper over the cheese. Bring the pastry end with no cheese up and fold over half the cheese pastry. Fold the remaining cheese pastry third over the rest of the pastry. Press down the edges of the pastry, then roll out again to a square 20 x 20 cm/8 x 8 in. Cut the square in half.

■ On one strip place two-thirds of the chopped olives, and on the other strip put two-thirds of the sun-dried tomatoes, covering the whole strip. For each strip, bring both long edges into the centre so that they meet in the middle. Flatten with a rolling pin and roll out a little.

■ Arrange the remaining one-third of each mixture over the pastry, and fold up again from both long edges to meet in the centre.

■ With a sharp knife, cut into 6-mm/¼-in strips. Place on a greased baking tray, leaving room to expand. Bake in the preheated oven for about 10 minutes, until golden brown. Serve warm.

Makes approx. 24 palmiers

Opposite: Deep-fried fresh vegetable chips (see page 78) and Olive and sun-dried tomato palmiers

DEEP-FRIED FRESH
VEGETABLE CHIPS

TIP
■

Serve these 'chips' on their own or as crudités to go with the dips on page 74. They can also be served with a main dish at a dinner party and always make an interesting talking point.

W hy buy ready-made, oversalted crisps when you can easily make your own with a variety of vegetables?

juice of 1 lemon
1 large potato
1 sweet potato
1 carrot
1 parsnip

225 g /8 oz celeriac
2 Jerusalem artichokes
1 beetroot
groundnut oil, for deep frying
salt

■ Have a large bowl of iced water ready, into which you have stirred the lemon juice.

■ Peel all the vegetables and slice very thinly. Use a food processor (slicing disk attachment) or a mandolin to make the slices really thin and even. Drop all the vegetable slices, except the beetroot (it will stain all the other vegetables), into the iced lemon water.

■ Drain and dry all the vegetables well on kitchen paper before cooking. Heat the oil in a wok until a cube of bread dropped in rises immediately to the surface and browns in less than a minute. Fry the vegetable slices in batches until crisp. Drain well and sprinkle with salt.

■ These chips can be reheated on a baking sheet in a preheated oven at 220°C/425°F/Gas Mark 7 for a few minutes before serving.

Serves 6

CHEESY LEEK AND
SWEET POTATO TORTILLA

Tortillas can be served at any temperature — hot, room temperature or cold, depending on the time of year. This one, which is rather like a pastry-less quiche, makes an excellent supper dish as well as being party food.

225 g/8 oz parsnips, peeled and chopped into small pieces
1 sweet potato, peeled and chopped into small pieces
2 leeks, trimmed, washed and shredded
6 free-range eggs
4 spring onions, finely chopped
salt and freshly ground black pepper
175 g/6 oz vegetarian Stilton, grated or crumbled
25 g/1 oz butter

> ### TIP
> ■
> Try to get an orange sweet potato as this gives extra colour to the dish. Butternut squash also makes a good alternative.

■ Preheat the oven to 180°C/350°F/Gas Mark 4.

■ Cook the parsnips and sweet potato together in boiling water until tender. Drain and cool. Steam the leeks for 3 minutes, then drain and cool.

■ Beat the eggs, then add the sweet potato, parsnips and leeks, the chopped spring onions and seasoning to taste.

■ Butter an ovenproof dish and put half the mixture into it. Sprinkle with the Stilton, then add the rest of the egg mixture.

■ Cover with greased foil and bake in the preheated oven for 40 minutes. Remove the foil and cook for a further 20-30 minutes, until the tortilla feels set and is golden in colour. Cut into wedges and serve with a crisp green salad.

Serves 8

ASPARAGUS AND
CASHEW MINI TARTLETS

TIP

■

The pastry can be
flavoured with a pinch of
dried mixed herbs or, for
a non-vegan version, add
50 g/2 oz grated
vegetarian Cheddar.

Asparagus is in season in early summer and has a very fresh
'green' flavour. When not in season you could use canned
asparagus, but treat it gently as it tends to be very soft.

225 g/8 oz plain white flour
pinch of salt
100 g/4 oz vegan margarine
4–6 tablespoons cold water
1 tablespoon vegetable oil
1 small onion, finely chopped
100 g/4 oz fresh asparagus tips, steamed until tender
50 g/2 oz cashew nuts, toasted and chopped
1 tablespoon shoyu
salt and freshly ground black pepper
parsley sprigs, to garnish

■ Preheat the oven to 200°C/400°F/Gas Mark 6.
■ Put the flour and salt in a bowl. Rub in the margarine with your fingertips to
resemble breadcrumbs. Mix in enough cold water to make a smooth, firm
dough. Roll into a ball, wrap in cling film and refrigerate for 30 minutes.
■ Heat the oil in a saucepan and fry the onion until golden. Chop the
asparagus and add to the onion with the cashew nuts. Stir in the shoyu, season
to taste with salt and pepper and cool.
■ Roll out the pastry to 2.5 mm/⅛ in thick. Use a pastry cutter to make
twelve 8-cm/3-in circles. Place in a greased patty pan. Prick the surface and
bake 'blind' (filled with baking beans) in the preheated oven for 10 minutes,
until the pastry shells are golden and crisp.
■ Cool on a wire rack. Spoon in
the asparagus and cashew
filling and serve garnished
with parsley sprigs.

Makes 12

STUFFED
BAKED POTATOES

There are many recipes for baked potato toppings, but removing the cooked flesh, mashing and mixing it with a filling and then reheating the filled shells is more practical for a party as well as being more tasty. As an alternative, use the Crostini toppings on page 36.

6 medium baking potatoes, scrubbed	1 tomato, skinned and chopped
olive oil, for baking	1 tablespoon lemon juice
1 red pepper	2 tablespoons chopped fresh
50 g/2 oz butter or vegan margarine*	coriander
a little milk or soya milk*	1 tablespoon olive oil
100 g/4 oz olives, stoned and chopped	100 g/4 oz mushrooms, chopped
salt and freshly ground black pepper	1 garlic clove, crushed
1 avocado, peeled, stoned and chopped	

- Preheat the oven to 200°C/400°F/Gas Mark 6.
- Rub the baking potatoes with the olive oil and prick all over with a fork. Place on a baking sheet and cook in the preheated oven for 45-60 minutes, until tender when pierced with a knife.
- At the same time, roast the red pepper until the skin is blistered and blackening. Put the pepper into a plastic bag and seal until cool enough to handle. Remove the skin and seeds and chop the flesh.
- Remove the potatoes from the oven, cut in half and spoon the flesh into a bowl. Beat in the butter or vegan margarine* and enough milk or soya milk* to give a creamy texture. Divide between 3 bowls.
- Mix the red pepper with the chopped olives and season to taste. Stir into one of the bowls of potato and use to fill 4 of the potato skin halves.
- Mix the avocado, tomato, lemon juice and coriander and season to taste. Stir into one of the bowls of potato and use to fill 4 of the potato skin halves.
- Heat the olive oil in a saucepan and fry the mushrooms and garlic for a few minutes until tender. Season and stir into the final bowl of potato and use to fill the remaining potato skin halves.
- Reduce the oven temperature to 180°C/350°F/Gas Mark 4, and gently reheat the filled potatoes on a baking tray for about 20–30 minutes. Serve hot.

Serves 12

TIP

■

The juices from the roast peppers are well worth saving and using as part of a salad dressing as they impart a rich, sweet flavour.

FILLED ITALIAN
FOCACCIA BREAD

Focaccia is a delicious Italian bread — the original pizza base. This variation in which the filling is cooked inside the bread makes an excellent party piece!

2 teaspoons sugar
12 g /½ oz fresh yeast
225 ml/8 fl oz tepid water
225 g/8 oz strong white flour
pinch of salt
2 tablespoons olive oil
150 g/5 oz mozzarella cheese, sliced

few basil leaves, roughly torn
4 sun-dried tomatoes in oil, sliced
1 garlic clove, crushed
extra olive oil
12 olives, stoned
2-3 sprigs fresh rosemary
coarse sea salt

■ Preheat the oven to 220°C/425°F/Gas Mark 7.

■ Stir the sugar into the yeast and add a little of the measured tepid water. Leave in a warm place for 5–10 minutes, until bubbles appear on the surface.

■ Mix the flour and salt in a bowl. Pour in the yeast mixture and olive oil. Add enough tepid water, a little at time, to make a pliable but not sticky dough.

■ Knead for 10 minutes on a lightly floured worktop. Leave in an oiled covered bowl in a warm place for about 40–60 minutes, to double in size.

■ Punch the dough down, turn out onto a lightly floured work top and knead for 3 minutes. Halve the dough and roll each half out into a rough circle, about 2.5 mm/⅛ in thick. Grease a baking sheet with olive oil and put one piece of dough onto the oiled surface. Cover with slices of mozzarella cheese, basil leaves and sun-dried tomatoes.

■ Place the second piece of dough over the top. Make some dimples in the top of the focaccia with your fingers.

■ Mix the crushed garlic with some olive oil and brush over the top of the dough. Put some olives in the dimples, then sprinkle with rosemary and sea salt. Leave to prove for 20 minutes.

■ Bake in the preheated oven for 10 minutes. Reduce the oven temperature to 190°C/375°F/Gas Mark 5 and bake for another 15-20 minutes, until golden and evenly cooked. Serve cut into wedges.

LEEK AND MUSHROOM
VOL AU VENTS

Ever popular, these crisp little pastry cups with a tasty leek and mushroom filling are easily made vegan by using soya cream. Make sure that when you take the lids off the cooked pastry cases you remove as much of the pastry inside as possible to leave room for the filling. Fill right to the brim before putting the little hat on.

450 g/1 lb ready-made vegan puff pastry
1 tablespoon groundnut oil or olive oil
1 large leek, trimmed, washed and finely shredded
100 g/4 oz mushrooms, finely chopped
2–3 teaspoons shoyu

2.5-cm/1-in piece fresh ginger root, peeled and grated
salt and freshly ground black pepper
1 tablespoon plain flour
150 ml/5 fl oz dairy or soya cream*
25 g/1 oz cashew nuts, toasted and chopped
sprigs of parsley, to garnish

■ Preheat the oven to 225°C/450°F/Gas Mark 8.
■ Roll out the pastry to 5 mm/¼-in thick and, using a 7.5-cm/3-in pastry cutter, cut out 12 circles. With a 5-cm/2-in cutter, cut an inner circle part way through each (this will form the lid once cooked). Place on a baking sheet and cook in the preheated oven for about 5 minutes, until risen and golden. Cool on a wire rack, then remove the lids and some of the pastry from the centre.

■ Heat the oil in a saucepan and gently cook the leek until tender. Add the mushrooms and cook over a high heat to evaporate the liquid. Stir in the shoyu, grated ginger and seasoning.
■ Add the flour and cook, stirring, for 2 minutes. Stir in the cream or soya cream* and cook until thickened. Stir in the cashew nuts.
■ Reheat the vol au vent cases at 180°C/350°F/Gas Mark 4 for about 15 minutes. Heat the filling and spoon into the hot cases, top with the lids at an angle and pop a sprig of parsley into the sauce. Serve warm.

Makes 12

CREAMY MUSHROOM
CROUSTADES

Use any mushrooms that you like for this recipe — button, field, chestnut, oyster, shiitake — or a mixture. The contrast of the creamy sauce with the crisp base is wonderful.

12 thin slices wholemeal bread, crusts removed
olive oil, for brushing
25 g/1 oz butter or vegan margarine*
1 onion, finely chopped
1 garlic clove, crushed
450 g/1 lb mushrooms, sliced
300 ml/10 fl oz soured cream or soya cream*
salt and freshly ground black pepper
1 teaspoon paprika

■ Preheat the oven to 190°C/375°F/Gas Mark 5.
■ Brush both sides of each slice of bread with olive oil. Place in a jam tart tin, pushing each one down to form a hollow. Bake in the preheated oven for 10-15 minutes, until crisp.
■ Meanwhile, melt the butter or vegan margarine* in a frying pan and fry the onion and garlic until transluscent. Add the mushrooms and continue cooking for a further 5 minutes. Stir in the soured cream or soya cream* and season with salt and pepper.
■ Spoon into the croustade 'nests' and sprinkle with the paprika. Serve the croustades immediately while they are still hot.

Makes 12

TIP

■

Cauliflower cheese would make an alternative topping as would finely diced aubergine quickly fried with red pepper, onion and tomato, then stirred into the cream or soya cream and scattered with chopped fresh herbs.

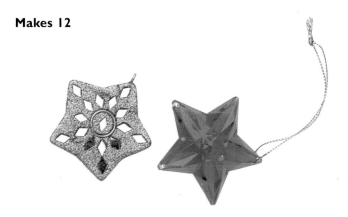

FESTIVE PARTY PUNCH

2 litres/3¼ pints vegetarian red
  wine
1 orange, sliced
1 lemon, sliced
100 g/4 oz sugar
1 piece cinnamon stick
6 whole cloves
1 piece dried ginger, bruised

½ tablespoon allspice berries
Cointreau (optional)

To garnish:
1 orange, sliced
1 lemon, sliced
2 apples, sliced
few sprigs of mint

■ Put all the ingredients (except the Cointreau, if using) into a large pan. Bring
to the boil, then remove from the heat and leave to stand for 2 hours.
■ Put ½ tablespoon of Cointreau in each serving glass, if using. Reheat the
punch, almost to boiling point, and transfer to a punch bowl. Garnish with
fresh fruit slices and sprigs of mint.
■ Pour into the glasses over the liqueur when the punch has cooled slightly.

Serves 12

WATERMELON AND STRAWBERRY PUNCH

1 watermelon
225 g/8 oz fresh strawberries,
  washed
crushed ice
2 bottles sparkling or dry white
  wine, chilled

1 bottle soda water, chilled

To garnish:
melon balls
strawberry halves
mint leaves

■ Peel and deseed the watermelon and hull the strawberries. Purée half of
the fruit in a liquidizer or food processor, then press through a sieve.
■ Transfer to a punch bowl with some of the crushed ice and add the
wine and soda water.
■ Make melon balls with a Parisienne baller and cut the reserved
strawberries in half. Add to the bowl with the mint leaves. Put the
remaining crushed ice in each wine glass as you serve the punch.

Serves 12–16

DINNER
PARTIES

SUMMER MENU   88

Fresh pea and mint soup with croûtons
Almond, coriander and cheese tuiles
Meringue stacks filled with summer fruits

FAR EASTERN MENU   93

Spiced mushroom satay
Thai vegetable curry with fragrant rice
Japanese green tea ice cream

INDIAN MENU   97

Spicy vegetable filo samosas
Paneer or tofu and vegetable moghlai
Kulfi

WINTER MENU   100

Cream cheese and herb pâté
Hazelnut and herb tarts filled with mushrooms
Apricot and pecan puddings with toffee sauce

Left: Paneer or tofu and vegetable moghlai (page 98) and Spicy vegetable filo samosas (page 97)

FRESH PEA AND MINT
SOUP WITH CROUTONS

The flavour of fresh garden peas conjures up long summer days and sunshine. If you are unable to obtain fresh peas or find shelling them too much trouble, then use frozen ones instead.

25 g/1 oz butter or vegan margarine*
1 onion, finely chopped
225 g/8 oz leeks, finely shredded and washed, keeping as much of the dark green as possible
225 g/8 oz potatoes, peeled and cut into small chunks
1.2 litres/2 pints light vegetable stock (use vegan bouillon powder)
225 g/8 oz fresh or frozen peas (weight without pod)

1 small bunch of mint, chopped
salt and freshly ground black pepper
single cream or soya cream*
mint sprigs, to garnish

Croûtons:
2 slices white bread
2 tablespoons olive oil
1 tablespoon chopped mint

■ Melt the butter or vegan margarine* in a saucepan and gently fry the onion until soft. Add the leeks and cook for a further 5 minutes.

■ Add the potatoes and stock, bring to the boil, then simmer, covered, for about 20 minutes, until the potatoes are tender. Add the peas and mint and simmer for a further 5 minutes.

■ Allow the soup to cool, then liquidize in a blender or food processor until very smooth. Return to a clean saucepan, reheat gently and season to taste with salt and pepper.

■ Serve the soup garnished with a swirl of single cream or soya cream*, a mint sprig and croûtons.

■ For the croûtons: mix the mint and olive oil together and season. Brush the bread on both sides with the oil and bake in a preheated oven at 200°C/400°F/Gas Mark 6 for 10-15 minutes, until crisp. Remove the crusts and cut into cubes.

Opposite: Fresh pea and mint soup with croûtons

ALMOND, CORIANDER
AND CHEESE TUILES

Tuiles are usually associated with desserts, filled with cream and fruit, but these savoury ones make a lovely alternative to a pastry base for holding grilled vegetables.

25 g/1 oz butter
25 g/1 oz plain white flour
$^{1}/_{2}$ teaspoon ground coriander
15 g/$^{1}/_{2}$ oz ground almonds
salt and freshly ground black pepper
2 free-range egg whites
25 g/1 oz vegetarian Parmesan or Pecorino, grated
fresh coriander and lemon zest

Artichoke filling:
450 g/1 lb can of artichokes, drained
2 red peppers
12 Kalamata olives, stoned and halved
1 tablespoon chopped fresh coriander
salt and freshly ground black pepper

Herb sauce:
150 ml/5 fl oz soured cream
juice of $^{1}/_{2}$ lemon
25 g/1 oz fresh coriander, chopped

■ Preheat the oven to 220°C/425°F/Gas Mark 7.
■ Melt the butter in a small saucepan. Sift the flour and ground coriander into a bowl. Mix in the ground almonds and season with salt and pepper.
■ Pour the melted butter and egg whites into the bowl and mix all the ingredients together with an electric hand mixer until you have a light batter.
■ Line a baking sheet with non-stick baking parchment. To make 2 tuiles, spoon 2 tablespoons of batter per portion onto the tray, spacing them well apart.
■ Smooth each spoonful out to a circle, about 15 cm/6 in diameter. Sprinkle with grated cheese and bake for 4 minutes in the preheated oven.
■ Remove the tray from the oven and immediately mould each biscuit over the base of a greased dariole mould to make a little basket (tuile). Replace the biscuits, still on their moulds, in the oven for 5–6 minutes and then unmould and cool. Repeat the process to make 4 tuiles in total.
■ For the filling: quarter the artichokes and grill until charred. Quarter the red peppers and grill, skin side up, until starting to blacken. Cool then remove the skin and seeds and chop. Mix together the peppers, artichokes, olives, coriander and seasoning.
■ Mix all the sauce ingredients or, for a greener sauce, whizz together in a blender.
■ Place a tuile on each serving plate. Fill with the artichoke mixture and drizzle a little of the sauce over the vegetables and onto the plate around the tuile. Garnish with fresh coriander leaves and lemon zest.

Opposite: Almond, coriander and cheese tuiles

MERINGUE STACKS
FILLED WITH SUMMER FRUITS

Y ou can use any combination of soft fruits with these meringues; to get the best flavours, opt for whatever is in season.

2 free-range egg whites
100 g / 4 oz caster sugar
sunflower or groundnut oil, for brushing
300 ml / 10 fl oz double or whipping cream
1 tablespoon Cointreau (or to taste)
225 g / 8 oz mixed summer fruits, e.g. strawberries, black grapes, peaches, kiwis, redcurrants

To garnish:
fanned strawberries
redcurrants
icing sugar, for dusting

- Preheat the oven to 130°C/250°F/Gas Mark ½.
- Whisk the egg whites in a grease-free bowl until stiff and dry. Whisk in half of the caster sugar, then fold in the remainder with a metal spoon.
- Draw eight 10-cm/4-in diameter circles on a sheet of baking parchment, place on a baking tray and brush each circle with a little oil. Divide the meringue evenly between the 8 circles and spread smoothly with a spatula.
- Bake in the preheated oven for 2 hours, until the meringue has dried out but without colouring. Remove from the tray and cool on a wire rack.
- Whip the cream until firm and then beat in the Cointreau. Wash and dry the fruit, slicing if necessary.
- Place 4 meringue circles on serving plates, spread evenly with the cream and arrange a mixture of the fruit on top. Cover with a second meringue circle, securing it in place with a little blob of cream in the centre. Arrange more fruit decoratively on top.
- Decorate the plate around each meringue stack with fanned strawberries and redcurrants. Dust with a little icing sugar and serve.

TIP
■
Try adding a few drops of vegetarian red food colouring to the egg whites with the sugar. This colours the meringue pink on the inside and makes a lovely contrast to the white of the outside and the cream, complementing the vivid colouring of the fruit.

SPICED MUSHROOM
SATAY

FAR EASTERN MENU

■

SERVES 4

■

Spiced mushroom satay

Thai vegetable curry with fragrant rice

Japanese green tea ice cream

Many recipes for satay sauce use peanut butter as a short cut. The flavour of the sauce is better, however, if whole ready roasted, unsalted peanuts are used and ground finely in a coffee grinder attachment.

225 g /8 oz fresh shiitake mushrooms (or soaked, dried mushrooms)

3 tablespoons chilli or garlic flavoured oil

4 slices wholemeal bread, toasted, cut into triangles and crusts removed

Satay sauce:

2 tablespoons groundnut oil

1 shallot, finely chopped

2 garlic cloves, crushed

2 large red chillies, deseeded and chopped

1 teaspoon grated fresh root ginger

1 tablespoon very finely chopped lemon grass

½ teaspoon salt

100 g /4 oz plain roasted peanuts, finely ground

200 ml /7 fl oz coconut milk

2 tablespoons dark muscovado sugar

1 tablespoon lime juice

freshly ground black pepper

■ Make the sauce: heat the groundnut oil in a saucepan and fry the shallot and garlic until starting to colour. Add the chillies, ginger, lemon grass and salt and cook for 2-3 minutes.

■ Add the peanuts, stir well to mix, then add the coconut milk and sugar. Bring to the boil and then simmer gently until the sauce thickens. Season with lime juice and black pepper and keep warm.

■ Remove the stalks from the mushrooms and cut each mushroom into quarters. Thread onto 4 soaked 15-cm/6-in long wooden skewers, brush well with the chilli or garlic oil and grill gently until cooked through.

■ Drizzle the satay sauce over the mushroom kebabs and serve hot with triangles of wholemeal toast.

THAI VEGETABLE
CURRY WITH FRAGRANT RICE

WINE SUGGESTIONS
■

White
Gewürztraminer
Pierre Frick
*An aromatic bouquet and
delightfully spicy flavour*

Red
Dominio los Piños Tinto
*Warm and supple
Spanish red*

Lemon grass, coriander, chillies, coconut milk — all these flavours belong to the wonderful food of Thailand. This curry is based on the traditional Thai green curry found in many restaurants.

225 g/8 oz Thai fragrant rice
grated lime zest
1 tablespoon chopped fresh
    lemon grass
1 garlic clove, crushed
½ bunch Thai basil
½ bunch fresh coriander, chopped
1–2 small (hot) red chillies, deseeded
    and finely chopped
4–5 tablespoons water
½ teaspoon black peppercorns
2 tablespoons groundnut oil
100 g/4 oz shallots or red onions,
    halved and sliced

1 garlic clove, crushed
1 small aubergine, cut into
    1-cm/½-in cubes
1 courgette, cut into
    1-cm/½-in cubes
100 g/4 oz green beans, cut into
    2.5-cm/1-in slices
100 g/4 oz mange tout, topped and
    tailed
300 ml/½ pint coconut milk
juice of ½ lime or lemon
salt and freshly ground black pepper
Thai basil and fresh coriander, to
    garnish

■ Cook the rice according to the instructions on the packet. Drain well, stir in the lime zest and keep warm.

■ Meanwhile, blend the lemon grass, garlic, basil, coriander, chillies, water and black peppercorns to a paste.

■ Heat the oil in a saucepan and gently fry the shallots or onions, garlic and aubergine for 5 minutes. Add the aromatic paste and cook over a gentle heat for 2 minutes.

■ Add the other vegetables and coconut milk and simmer for 15–20 minutes, until cooked. Add the lime or lemon juice, salt and pepper.

■ Serve the curry with the Thai fragrant rice, garnished with sprigs of Thai basil and fresh coriander.

*Opposite: Thai vegetable
curry with fragrant rice*

JAPANESE GREEN
TEA ICE CREAM

Japanese green tea powder is used to flavour this unusual and delicious ice cream. Serve with seasonal and colourful fruits to make a visual contrast to the bright green of the ice cream. Green tea powder can be purchased in Asian and Oriental food stores.

1½ tablespoons green tea powder
100 g / 4 oz caster sugar
300 ml / ½ pint milk
4 free-range egg yolks
1½ tablespoons cornflour
few drops of vanilla essence
225 ml / 8 fl oz whipping cream
raspberries and redcurrants, to serve

■ Mix the green tea powder and 1 tablespoon of the caster sugar together in a bowl.

■ Gently heat the milk in a saucepan to blood heat, then pour gradually onto the green tea powder, stirring all the time. Sieve to remove any lumps.

■ Beat the egg yolks and remaining sugar together until pale and creamy. Stir into the green tea mixture. Sift the cornflour over the liquid and fold in gently with the vanilla essence.

■ Return to the saucepan and heat gently, stirring with a wooden spoon, until thick and creamy. Cool.

■ Whip the cream to the soft peak stage, then fold into the mixture. Either churn in an ice cream machine, following the manufacturer's instructions, or turn into a metal bowl and freeze for about 3–4 hours, whisking the partially frozen ice cream twice during this time.

■ Serve the ice cream, decorated with raspberries and redcurrants or other fruit of your choice.

TIP

■

Japanese food always looks wonderful served on black china. The raspberries or redcurrants can be 'frosted' by dipping into a little egg white and then into caster sugar.

SPICY VEGETABLE
FILO SAMOSAS

INDIAN MENU

■

SERVES 4

■

Spicy vegetable filo samosas

Paneer or tofu and vegetable moghlai

Kulfi

*CAN BE VEGAN

Use left-over potatoes and other vegetables to vary the filling in these mildly spicy samosas. Samosas can be eaten as a snack food too and are good for a buffet dish at any time of the year.

1 tablespoon groundnut oil
1 onion, finely chopped
2 garlic cloves, crushed
1 green chilli, deseeded and chopped
2.5-cm/1-in piece of fresh root ginger, peeled and grated
1 teaspoon cumin seeds
1 teaspoon ground coriander
½ teaspoon turmeric
3 tablespoons chopped fresh coriander

pinch of salt
juice of ½ lemon
100 g/4 oz potatoes, finely chopped and steamed
200 g/7 oz can of processed peas, drained
1 packet filo pastry
25 g/1 oz butter or vegan margarine*, melted
selection of chutneys and raitas, to serve

■ Preheat the oven to 190°C/375°F/Gas Mark 5.
■ Heat the oil in a frying pan and fry the onion and garlic until soft. Add the chilli, ginger, spices, fresh coriander, salt and lemon juice. Stir well to mix. Add the cooked potatoes and peas. Mix well and leave to cool.
■ Cut the filo sheets into 9 cm x 30 cm/4 x 12 in strips. Use 2 strips at a time, keeping the rest covered with a clean damp cloth.
■ Brush one strip lightly with melted butter or vegan margarine* and place the second strip on top. Brush again. Place 1½ tablespoons of the samosa mixture at one end of the strip.
■ Fold the end of the pastry over the filling, making a triangular shape, and continue folding up the strip to the top, alternating diagonal and straight folds to maintain the triangular shape. Repeat with the rest of the pastry and mixture until all of it is used up.
■ Brush the samosas with melted butter or vegan margarine*. Place on an oiled baking sheet and bake in the preheated oven for about 20 minutes, until crisp and golden.
■ Serve the samosas with mango chutney, lime pickle and cucumber raita (yogurt mixed with chopped cucumber and fresh mint).

*CAN BE VEGAN

PANEER OR TOFU
AND VEGETABLE MOGHLAI

DRINKS TIP
■

Spicy aromatic white wines, especially Gewürztraminer from Alsace, Irsai Oliver from Hungary and fruity dry Muscats, complement Indian food. Alternatively, a good-quality premium lager may be preferred.

Rich, creamy and delicately spicy are the attributes that characterize this style of cooking. Paneer is an Indian cheese which is stocked by many supermarkets and is similar in texture to a firm block of tofu; both keep their shape and texture when cooked.

2.5-cm/1-in piece fresh root ginger, peeled and grated

4 garlic cloves, crushed

50 g/2 oz ground almonds

6–8 tablespoons water

2 tablespoons groundnut oil

225 g/8 oz paneer or plain tofu*, cut into 2.5-cm/1-in pieces

10 whole cardamom pods

2.5-cm/1-in stick cinnamon

6 whole cloves

1 tablespoon whole coriander seeds

2 teaspoons whole cumin seeds

1 onion, finely chopped

1 green chilli, deseeded and finely chopped

100 g/4 oz green beans, sliced into 2.5-cm/1-in pieces

1 courgette, sliced

300 ml/10 fl oz single cream or soya cream*

50 g/2 oz sultanas

salt, to taste

25 g/1 oz toasted flaked almonds, to garnish

■ In a bowl, blend the ginger, garlic, ground almonds and water together to make a smooth paste.

■ Heat the oil in a frying pan and gently cook the paneer or tofu* until golden on both sides. Drain on kitchen paper and set aside.

■ Put the whole spices into the same oil and cook for 2 minutes. Add the onion and chilli and cook until golden. Add the ginger paste, green beans and courgette and cook for a further 2 minutes.

■ Stir in the cream and paneer or tofu* and soya cream* and simmer for 10–15 minutes, until the vegetables are cooked. Stir in the sultanas. Add salt to taste.

■ Garnish with toasted almonds and serve with boiled rice.

KULFI

The Indian equivalent of ice cream, this is a very refreshing dessert to serve after a spicy meal. The flavours can be complemented by serving cardamom tea or coffee at the end of the meal.

900 ml/1 ½ pints full-cream milk
4 whole cardamom pods
75 g/3 oz soft brown sugar
25 g/1 oz ground almonds
150 ml/5 fl oz double cream
25 g/1 oz pistachio nuts, chopped
chopped pistachio nuts, to decorate

■ Place the milk and cardamom pods in a heavy-based saucepan and bring to the boil. Lower the heat and simmer gently for about 1 hour, until the milk has reduced in volume by half.

■ Add the sugar, stirring until dissolved, then strain into a bowl and add the ground almonds. Leave to cool. Stir the double cream and pistachios into the cold mixture.

■ Use an ice cream maker (following the manufacturer's instructions) or freeze in a metal bowl until mushy. Beat with an electric hand whisk and then freeze again until solid.

■ Transfer the kulfi to the refrigerator 30 minutes before serving. Scoop out and serve decorated with chopped pistachio nuts.

Right: Paneer or tofu and vegetable moghlai

CREAM CHEESE AND HERB PATE

This is a very simple pâté to prepare. It can be made in advance and kept in the refrigerator for 24 hours before your dinner party. You can use other herbs or nuts — in fact, any combination that you fancy. This pâté makes a good sandwich filling too or can be used for filling sticks of celery, quarters of pepper or cherry tomato halves for finger buffets.

225 g/8 oz cream cheese (for low-fat version use Quark)
50 g/2 oz walnuts, ground
1 tablespoon chopped fresh flat-leaf parsley
1 tablespoon chopped fresh chives
1 tablespoon chopped fresh tarragon
pinch of chilli powder
salt and freshly ground black pepper

To serve:
4 walnut halves
sprigs of herbs and chive flowers
pinch of paprika
melba toast

■ Beat the cream cheese in a bowl until it is smooth. Stir in all the other ingredients thoroughly and season to taste.
■ Spoon the pâté mixture into 4 individual ramekins, pressing down firmly. Refrigerate until required.
■ Garnish the top of each ramekin with a walnut half. Place each ramekin on a serving plate and decorate the plates with sprigs of herbs, chive flowers and a sprinkling of paprika. Serve with melba toast.

HAZELNUT AND HERB
TARTS FILLED WITH MUSHROOMS

Individual tarts are more appealing for a special occasion than cutting slices from a large one. These tarts look lovely presented on a white plate in a circle of colourful mixed salad leaves with a drizzle of lemony vinaigrette.

200 g / 7 oz plain flour
pinch of salt
100 g / 4 oz butter, cubed
50 g / 2 oz hazelnuts, chopped and
 roasted
1 tablespoon chopped fresh thyme
 or rosemary
1 free-range egg yolk
2–3 tablespoons iced water

2 garlic cloves, crushed
225 g / 8 oz exotic mushrooms,
 e.g. mixed oyster, shiitake, field
 and straw mushrooms, sliced
 fairly thickly
300 ml / 10 fl oz crème fraîche
1 tablespoon chopped fresh thyme
 or rosemary
salt and freshly ground black pepper

Mushroom filling:
225 g / 8 oz shallots, quartered
2 tablespoons groundnut oil
1 tablespoon soft brown sugar

To garnish:
sliced button mushrooms
pinch of paprika
chopped fresh parsley

**WINE
SUGGESTIONS**
■

White
Domaine St Michel
Chardonnay
Full fruited, crisp dry white

Red
Domaine Cabrairal
Corbières
*Fairly robust and well
balanced Midi red*

■ Preheat the oven to 200°C/400°F/Gas Mark 6.

■ Sift the flour and salt into a bowl. Cut the butter into small pieces and rub in until the mixture resembles breadcrumbs. Stir in the hazelnuts and herbs and mix with the egg yolk and iced water to make a smooth dough. Knead briefly, then wrap in cling film and refrigerate for 30 minutes.

■ Cook the shallots gently in the oil for about 10 minutes. Stir in the sugar and garlic and continue cooking until the shallots are golden and soft. Add the mushrooms and cook for 5 minutes, stirring all the time. Take off the heat, cool and add the crème fraîche, herbs and seasoning.

■ Roll out the pastry and cut to fit 4 individual 10-cm/4-in loose-bottomed flan tins. Prick the bases and refrigerate for 30 minutes.

■ Bake the pastry cases 'blind' (filled with baking beans) for 15 minutes in the preheated oven. Reduce the heat to 180°C/350°F/Gas Mark 4. Fill with the mushroom mixture and bake for 15 minutes.

■ Turn the tarts out of the tins and garnish with a sliced button mushroom, a sprinkling of paprika and some chopped parsley.

APRICOT AND PECAN
PUDDINGS WITH TOFFEE SAUCE

TIP

■

Pear and hazelnut or plum and almond are also delicious combinations which can be substituted in these puddings. Use almond essence in place of vanilla to intensify the nutty flavour.

There is a great combination of textures in these very light puddings, which are served with a delicious toffee sauce.

50 g /2 oz light muscovado sugar
50 g /2 oz pecan nuts, chopped
100 g /4 oz ready-to-eat dried
 apricots, chopped
pecan nut halves, to garnish

Almond base:
75 g /3 oz butter or vegan margarine*
60 ml /2 fl oz maple syrup or soft
 brown sugar
1 free-range egg, beaten or
 1 tablespoon soya flour mixed
 with 2 tablespoons water*

75 g /3 oz ground almonds
25 g /1 oz soya flour
1/2 teaspoon baking powder
few drops of vanilla essence

Toffee sauce:
200 g /7 oz light muscovado sugar
90 ml /3 fl oz double cream or soya
 cream*
100 g /4 oz unsalted butter or vegan
 margarine*
1/2 teaspoon vanilla essence
25 g /1 oz chopped pecan nuts

■ Preheat the oven to 180°C/350°F/Gas Mark 4.

■ To make the topping, mix the sugar, chopped pecans and dried apricots together. Divide equally between 4 well-greased, individual ramekins.

■ Cream the butter or margarine* for the base with the maple syrup or sugar. Add the egg or soya flour paste* and mix well. Stir in the almonds, soya flour, baking powder and vanilla essence.

■ Spoon the mixture into the ramekins, place on a baking tray and bake in the preheated oven for 20–30 minutes

■ Make the sauce: put the sugar in a saucepan and use a wooden spoon to crush any lumps. Add the cream and butter (or soya cream* and vegan margarine*) and stir together over a gentle heat until the butter has melted. Bring to the boil and simmer for 2-3 minutes, until toffee-coloured. Remove from the heat, then stir in the vanilla essence and chopped pecans.

■ Turn each pudding out onto a serving plate. Decorate with pecan halves. Spoon a little toffee sauce around the puddings and serve immediately.

Opposite: Apricot and pecan pudding with toffee sauce

DESSERTS

*Left: Chocolate espresso and roasted pecan tarte (page 125)
and Lemon curd profiteroles (page 111)*

PEAR AND STEM
GINGER SORBET

Ginger comes in many forms: fresh root, pickled, ground and preserved in syrup. All are delicious and there is no better combination than pear and ginger.

675 g/1½ lb pears, peeled, cored and sliced
450 ml/15 fl oz water
175 g/6 oz caster sugar
1 tablespoon lemon juice
2 pieces stem ginger in syrup, finely chopped
1 tablespoon stem ginger syrup
mint sprigs, to garnish
strawberry halves, to garnish

■ Stew the pears in the water until soft. Drain the pears, reserving the liquid, and purée the fruit.
■ Fast boil the reserved liquid to reduce it to 300 ml/½ pint. Stir in the sugar until dissolved, bring to the boil and boil for 3–4 minutes to make a sugar syrup.
■ Add all the other ingredients and pour into a polythene or metal container.
■ Cool, then freeze uncovered until half frozen. Mash the mixture well to break up any icy particles and return to the freezer until solid. Alternatively, use an ice cream maker (following the manufacturer's instructions).
■ Remove from the freezer 10–20 minutes before serving, mashing with a fork to break up the crystals. Shape the sorbet between 2 spoons or use a scoop and place in sundae dishes. Garnish with mint sprigs and strawberry halves.

Serves 4

TIP

■

Sorbets are very refreshing at the end of a summer meal. This one is lovely served with Florentines (see page 123).

SPICY TOFFEE APPLE
ICE CREAM

Toffee apples are a traditional part of Hallowe'en. This is a way in which adults can indulge in these sweet flavours without the stickiness of an apple covered in toffee. Why wait for Hallowe'en anyway — this recipe is good to serve all year round.

300 ml/½ pint full cream milk
300 ml/10 fl oz double cream
1 vanilla pod, split lengthways
6 medium free-range egg yolks
175 g/6 oz caster sugar
450 g/1 lb dessert apples, peeled,
    cored and chopped
2 tablespoons lemon juice

½–1 teaspoon ground cinnamon or
    mixed spice (optional)
75 g/3 oz vegetarian toffees, cut
    into pieces

To garnish:
mint leaves
lemon zest curls

■ Put the milk, cream and vanilla pod in a saucepan and bring to the boil. Remove from the heat and leave the flavours to infuse for 15 minutes. Strain and discard the vanilla pod and seeds.

■ Whisk the egg yolks and sugar together in a bowl until pale and fluffy. Then whisk in the vanilla cream and pour the mixture into a clean saucepan. Cook over a very low heat, stirring all the time, until the mixture thickens and coats the back of a wooden spoon. Remove from the heat and allow to cool.

■ Place the prepared apples in a saucepan with the lemon juice and cook over a low heat until soft. Mash and leave to cool. Stir in the spices, if using.

■ Stir the toffee pieces and apples into the custard and pour into a shallow polythene container. Freeze for 30 minutes, then beat with a fork. Repeat this process, then freeze until hard (alternatively, use an ice cream making machine, following the manufacturer's instructions).

■ Take out of the freezer for 30 minutes before serving. Scoop into sundae dishes and decorate with mint leaves and lemon zest curls.

Serves 4

LEMON CURD
ICE CREAM

To make a quicker ice cream that does not need beating during the freezing process, use 450 ml/¾ pint each of whipped double cream and Greek yogurt. Fold together with 175 g/6 oz icing sugar and a few drops of vanilla essence. Fold in the lemon curd and turn into a polythene container and freeze until solid.

300 ml/½ pint full-cream milk
300 ml/½ pint double cream
1 vanilla pod, split lengthways
6 medium free-range egg yolks
175 g/6 oz caster sugar
mint leaves and lemon zest curls,
    to garnish

For the lemon curd:
juice and grated zest of 1 lemon
1 large free-range egg
35 g/1½ oz caster sugar
25 g/1 oz unsalted butter, cut into
    small pieces

■ Make the lemon curd first. Whisk the lemon juice and egg together in a bowl.

■ In a separate bowl, mix together the lemon zest and sugar. Pour the whisked egg over the sugar and add the butter.

■ Place the bowl over a pan of simmering water, stirring frequently with a wooden spoon until thick. Leave to cool.

■ Make the ice cream. Put the milk, cream and vanilla pod into a saucepan and bring to the boil. Remove from the heat and leave the flavours to infuse for 15 minutes. Strain and discard the vanilla pod and seeds.

■ Whisk the egg yolks and sugar together in a bowl until pale and fluffy. Then whisk in the vanilla cream and pour the mixture into a clean saucepan.

■ Cook over a very low heat, stirring all the time, until the mixture thickens and coats the back of a wooden spoon. Remove from the heat and allow to cool.

■ Stir the lemon curd into the custard and pour into a shallow polythene container. Freeze for 30 minutes, then beat with a fork. Repeat this process, then freeze until hard (alternatively, use an ice cream making machine, following the manufacturer's instructions).

■ Take the ice cream out of the freezer for 30 minutes before serving. Scoop into sundae dishes and decorate with mint leaves and lemon zest curls.

Serves 4

Opposite: Lemon curd ice cream

*CAN BE VEGAN

SHORTBREAD TARTS
WITH FRESH FRUIT

TIP
■
Substitute 50 g/2 oz
finely ground roasted
hazelnuts for 50 g/2 oz of
the plain flour to give the
pastry a nutty flavour.

This is a very summery dessert and would be a lovely finish to an
al fresco meal. Assemble the tarts just before serving to prevent
the pastry becoming soggy.

100 g/4 oz butter or vegan margarine*
175 g/6 oz white flour
50 g/2 oz soft brown muscovado
   sugar
1–2 tablespoons milk or soya milk*
100 g/4 oz strawberries, sliced
2 kiwi fruit, sliced
100 g/4 oz blueberries
icing sugar and mint leaves, to decorate

Crème patissière:
300 ml/½ pint soya milk
1 vanilla pod
2 heaped tablespoons vegan custard
   powder
2 tablespoons caster sugar
½ teaspoon vanilla essence
100 ml/4 fl oz soya cream

■ Preheat the oven to 150°C/300°F/Gas Mark 2.

■ Rub the butter or vegan margarine* into the flour until it resembles
breadcrumbs. Add the sugar and mix well. Work the mixture together to form
a firm dough, adding a little milk or soya milk* if necessary. Press into 4
individual (or one 20-cm/8-in) flan ring(s), moulding the dough up the sides.
Bake in the preheated oven for about 35–45 minutes. Cool, then turn out
onto a serving dish.

■ To make the crème patissière, heat the soya milk to boiling point in a
saucepan. Add a vanilla pod, turn off the heat and set aside for 30 minutes.
Place the custard powder and caster sugar in a bowl. Mix to a paste with a
little of the soya milk.

■ Remove the vanilla pod from the remaining soya milk, and return to the
boil. Pour onto the custard powder paste, stir well and return to the pan.
Bring to the boil, stirring continuously. Reduce the heat to a simmer and cook
for a further 2 minutes, until it thickens. Remove from the heat, stir in the
vanilla essence and soya cream. Cool completely.

■ Spoon the crème patissière into the shortbread cases. Decorate with the
prepared fruit. Dust with icing sugar and decorate with sprigs of mint.

Serves 4

LEMON CURD
PROFITEROLES

I always make my own lemon curd as most of the ready-made ones contain battery eggs — it also tastes better and is quite quick and easy, which is just as well as a batch never lasts very long.

150 ml/¼ pint water
50 g/2 oz butter
pinch of salt
65 g/2½ oz plain white flour (in a jug)
2 large free-range eggs, beaten
100 g/4 oz icing sugar, sifted
juice of ½–1 lemon
150 ml/5 fl oz single or double cream

Lemon curd:
zest and juice of 2 lemons
2 large free-range eggs
75 g/3 oz caster sugar
50 g/2 oz unsalted
   butter cut into
   small pieces

■ Preheat the oven to 220°C/425°F/Gas Mark 7.
■ Make the lemon curd first. Whisk the lemon juice and eggs together in a bowl. In a separate bowl, mix together the lemon zest and sugar. Pour the eggs over the sugar and add the butter. Place over a pan of simmering water, stirring frequently with a wooden spoon, until thick. Leave to cool.
■ Put the water, butter and salt for the choux pastry in a saucepan and heat until the water is just boiling and the butter has melted.
■ Remove from the heat and add all the flour at once by pouring it from the jug. Beat to form a shiny dough, then return to the heat and cook for 2 minutes, stirring frequently until you have a ball of dough in the centre of the pan.
■ Add the beaten egg, a little at a time, beating well between each addition. You should have a glossy dough of piping consistency. The more you beat at this stage, the lighter and crisper the pastry will be.
■ Either spoon the choux pastry onto a parchment-lined baking sheet, a tablespoon at a time, or put the mixture into a piping bag with a large nozzle and pipe 'blobs'. Bake in the preheated oven for 15 minutes, then reduce the heat to 190°C/375°F/Gas Mark 5 for a further 10-15 minutes, until crisp and golden.
■ Remove from the oven, and slit each profiterole to allow the steam to escape. Cool on a wire rack, then fill with lemon curd.
■ Mix the icing sugar and lemon juice to make a thin glacé icing.
Pile the profiteroles up on a dish and drizzle the lemon icing over the top. Serve with cream.

Serves 4 (makes 12 profiteroles)

NECTARINE AND
PHYSALIS CREAM PIE

Fresh nectarines are only available for a short season. You can substitute other fruit in this pie — pears work especially well if you use almond essence in place of vanilla in the custard cream.

50 g/2 oz butter
100 g/4 oz plain white flour
2 teaspoons soft brown sugar
2–3 tablespoons chilled water
4-6 physalis, opened out to expose
   the fruit, to garnish

Fruit filling:
300 ml/½ pint milk
2 free-range egg yolks, lightly beaten
2 teaspoons sugar

few drops of vanilla essence
grated zest of ½ lemon
2 teaspoons plain white flour
3 tablespoons extra thick double
   cream
4 ripe nectarines, stoned and sliced
100 g/4 oz physalis halved

Meringue topping:
2 free-range egg whites
100 g/4 oz caster sugar

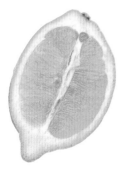

■ Preheat the oven to 200°C/400°F/Gas Mark 6.
■ Rub the butter into the flour to resemble breadcrumbs. Stir in the sugar and mix to a dough with chilled water. Roll into a ball, wrap in cling film and refrigerate for 30 minutes.
■ Roll out the dough to fit a 20-cm/8-in flan ring, then bake 'blind' (filled with baking beans) for 5–10 minutes. Remove from the oven and reduce the heat to 120°C/250°F/Gas Mark ½.
■ Make the filling. Bring the milk to the boil. In a bowl, mix the egg yolks, sugar, vanilla essence, lemon zest and flour. Pour the boiled milk into the bowl and mix well. Return to the saucepan and heat gently, stirring, until thickened. When cool, stir in the double cream.
■ Pour the custard into the part-cooked flan case. Arrange slices of nectarine and halved physalis on top.
■ Whip the egg whites in a grease-free bowl, then add the sugar, a tablespoon at at time, whisking until you have a meringue. Spread over the top of the flan.
■ Place on a baking tray and bake gently for about 1 hour.
■ Allow to go cold, then place the pie overnight (about 8 hours) in the refrigerator, so that the filling becomes firm. Serve decorated with the extra physalis.

Serves 4–6

FRESH SUMMER
FRUIT BRULEE

This dish can be prepared in advance and the sugar on the topping caramelized just before serving. Ideal as the finish to an *al fresco* meal, the sugar will still be bubbling as you carry it into the garden. The vegan topping makes a delicious alternative to the more traditional dairy version.

100 g/4 oz strawberries, halved
50 g/2 oz seedless green grapes, halved
½ melon, flesh scooped out into balls
2 ripe peaches, stoned and sliced
2 kiwi fruit, peeled and sliced
100 g/4 oz black cherries
3–4 tablespoons Cointreau
10 vegetarian macaroons or other
    crumbly biscuits

For the topping:
200 ml/7 fl oz Greek yogurt

200 ml/7 fl oz crème fraîche
100 g/4 oz light brown soft sugar

For the vegan* topping:
175 g/6 oz ground almonds
150 ml/¼ pint water
maple syrup, to taste
150 ml/¼ pint soya cream

To decorate:
8 strawberries, halved and fanned
few sprigs of mint

TIP
■
If you have tall sundae glasses, layer the fruit, biscuits and topping in each glass and chill. Just before serving, gently melt the sugar with 2–3 tablespoons of water in a saucepan and bring to the boil, stirring continuously. Boil until caramelized, then drizzle a little over each serving.

■ Place the prepared fruit in the base of a 900-ml/1½-pint ovenproof dish and drizzle with Cointreau. Crumble the macaroons or other biscuits over the top of the fruit.

■ Mix the yogurt and crème fraîche together and spoon over to seal in the fruit completely. Chill in the refrigerator for at least 1 hour. If making the vegan topping, place all the ingredients in a blender and blend until smooth. Spoon over the fruit as before.

■ Sprinkle the sugar over the topping and place under a preheated hot grill for 2–3 minutes, until the sugar melts and bubbles.

■ Serve decorated with fanned strawberry halves and mint sprigs.

Serves 4–6

*CAN BE VEGAN

APRICOT CHOCOLATE
REFRIGERATOR CAKE

This is a grown-up variation of 'Tiffin', the 'no cook' chocolate, fruit and biscuit cake. The Amaretto liqueur makes it really special. At Christmas you can buy apricots bottled in Amaretto, but it is easy enough to marinate dried apricots in the liqueur for a few hours before making the cake.

100 g / 4 oz good quality plain vegan chocolate
100 g / 4 oz butter or vegan margarine*
2 tablespoons golden syrup
1 tablespoon milk or soya milk*
250 g / 9 oz vegan digestive or almond biscuits, crushed
100 g / 4 oz apricots in Amaretto liqueur
50 g / 2 oz chopped roast hazelnuts or almonds
sliced apricots, to decorate
150 ml / 5 fl oz double cream, whipped (omit for vegans*)

Apricot coulis:
100 g / 4 oz canned apricots, drained
1 teaspoon Amaretto liqueur

■ Melt the chocolate in a bowl over a saucepan of hot water.
■ In a separate bowl, also over a saucepan of simmering water, melt the butter or vegan margarine*, golden syrup and milk together.
■ Stir the melted chocolate and crushed biscuits into the golden syrup mixture and mix well. Add the apricots and nuts, and mix well.
■ Grease and line a 450-g/1-lb loaf tin with baking parchment. Spoon in the chocolate biscuit mixture, press down well and chill for 2 hours.
■ Make the coulis: purée the apricots and Amaretto in a blender or press through a sieve.
■ Serve the cake sliced with some apricot coulis, sliced apricots and whipped cream (optional).

Serves 6–8

Opposite: Apricot chocolate refrigerator cake

INDIVIDUAL APPLE
CHARLOTTES

TIP

■

If the apples are a little too sharp for your taste, stir a little sugar into the warm purée.

Nobody would guess that these little puddings are dairy- and egg-free. They make a light but filling winter dessert, the apple purée in the centre being an unexpected surprise.

225 g/8 oz Bramley apples, peeled, cored and sliced
2 tablespoons vegan sweet cider
grated zest and juice of 1 lemon
1/2 teaspoon ground cinnamon
75 g/3 oz soft vegan margarine
4 tablespoons maple syrup or soft brown sugar
1 tablespoon soya flour mixed with 2 tablespoons water

75 g/3 oz ground almonds
25 g/1 oz soya flour
1/2 teaspoon baking powder
1/2 teaspoon almond essence

To serve:
icing sugar, for dusting
4 strawberries
few sprigs of mint
soya cream

■ Preheat the oven to 180°C/350°F/Gas Mark 4.

■ Cook the apple slices in the cider and lemon juice. Add the lemon zest and cinnamon and purée well.

■ Cream the margarine with the maple syrup or sugar. Mix the soya flour and water together and stir into the creamed mixture.

■ Stir in the ground almonds, soya flour, baking powder and almond essence.

■ Grease 4 individual ramekins and divide two-thirds of the sponge mixture equally between them. Use a teaspoon to make an indentation in the centre and ease the mixture up the sides.

■ Put the apple purée into the centre of each sponge, leaving enough room to top each one with the remaining sponge mixture.

■ Place on a baking sheet and bake in the preheated oven for 15–20 minutes, until firm and golden.

■ Dust with icing sugar and decorate with strawberries and mint sprigs. Serve hot with soya cream.

Serves 4

MINCEMEAT AND APRICOT CRUMBLE TART

Vegetarian mincemeat is widely available in both basic and luxury versions. You can use a basic mincemeat in this recipe and transform it into a luxury one by the addition of the brandied apricots. This festive tart is equally delicious served hot or cold.

225 g/8 oz dried apricots
8 tablespoons brandy
225 g/8 oz ready-made shortcrust
  pastry
450-g/1-lb jar vegetarian mincemeat
225 g/8 oz Bramley apples, peeled
  and cored
juice of 1 lemon
toasted flaked almonds, to decorate

cream, crème fraîche, or soya
  cream*, to serve

Crumble topping:
50 g/2 oz plain flour
50 g/2 oz ground almonds
50 g/2 oz butter or vegan
  margarine*
50 g/2 oz soft brown sugar

TIP

Ready-made shortcrust pastry can be bought in most supermarkets. It is a great time saver in a busy festive season but, of course, you can make your own if you prefer.

■ Preheat the oven to 200°C/400°F/Gas Mark 6. Marinate the dried apricots in the brandy for at least 1 hour.

■ Roll out the pastry and use to line a 22-cm/9-in loose-bottomed flan ring. Prick the base with a fork and rest in the refrigerator for 30 minutes. Line with baking parchment and baking beans and bake 'blind' for about 10-15 minutes in the preheated oven. Remove from the oven and allow to cool a little.

■ Chop up the marinated apricots and stir into the mincemeat with any remaining brandy. Use to fill the base of the pastry case.

■ Slice the prepared apples, dip in lemon juice to prevent them discolouring and arrange on top of the mincemeat.

■ For the crumble topping: mix the flour and ground almonds in a bowl, rub in the butter or vegan margarine* and stir in the sugar.

■ Sprinkle the crumble topping on top of the apples and bake for 30–40 minutes, until golden.

■ Decorate with toasted almonds and serve with cream, crème fraîche or vegan soya cream*.

Serves 6

PEAR, BRANDY AND
HAZELNUT STRUDEL

Most strudel recipes use filo pastry. This one is different in that it uses very thinly rolled puff pastry which gives a richer and flakier result than filo and is easier to eat!

450 g / 1 lb dessert pears (Comice, Conference, Rocha or William)
50 g / 2 oz chopped roasted hazelnuts
25 g / 1 oz brown sugar
50 g / 2 oz sultanas
1/2 teaspoon ground cinnamon
1 tablespoon brandy
225 g / 8 oz ready-made puff pastry
25 g / 1 oz butter or vegan margarine*
icing sugar, for dusting

■ Preheat the oven to 200°C/400°F/Gas Mark 6.
■ Peel, core and chop the pears and mix in a bowl with the hazelnuts, sugar, sultanas, cinnamon and brandy.
■ Roll out the puff pastry very thinly — you should be able to see the pattern of the work top through it.
■ Melt the butter or vegan margarine* in a small saucepan and brush over the surface of the pastry. Place the filling at one narrow end and roll up, folding in the sides to enclose the filling as you go.
■ Place on a greased baking sheet, brush with more butter or margarine* and make a couple of cuts in the top.
■ Bake in the preheated oven for about 20 minutes, until the pastry is well risen and golden. Dust the strudel with icing sugar and serve hot with custard, cream or soya cream*.

Serves 4

TIP

An alternative way of using the hazelnuts in this recipe is to leave them out of the mixture and sprinkle them over the whole surface of the pastry which has been brushed with fat instead. When the strudel is rolled up, you get crunchy hazelnuts between each flaky layer of the pastry.

STICKY GINGER AND
LEMON SYRUP CAKE

This is a wonderfully sticky cake, partly because of the lemon syrup which is poured over and allowed to soak into the warm cake as it comes out of the oven. A spoonful of crème fraîche complements the flavour and freshens the palette.

225 g/8 oz self-raising flour
1/2 teaspoon bicarbonate of soda
2 teaspoons ground ginger
100 g/4 oz butter
4 tablespoons molasses
125 g/5 oz muscovado sugar
grated zest and juice of 1 lemon
1 free-range egg, beaten

2 tablespoons milk
2 pieces stem ginger in syrup,
  chopped

To serve:
quartered slices of lemon
crème fraîche

■ Preheat the oven to 180°C/350°F/Gas Mark 4.

■ In a bowl, sift the flour, bicarbonate of soda and ground ginger together.

■ Melt the butter in a saucepan with the molasses and 100 g/4 oz of the sugar. Cool slightly, then add the lemon zest and whisk in the egg and milk. Pour the liquid ingredients into the flour, then add the chopped ginger in syrup and beat well.

■ Turn into a greased and lined 900-g/2-lb loaf tin. Bake in the preheated oven for 40–45 minutes, until risen and firm to the touch.

■ Warm the lemon juice in a saucepan and stir in the remaining 25 g/1 oz sugar until dissolved. Pierce the top of the cake with a skewer and pour the syrup over the cake. Leave to cool, then turn out.

■ Decorate the cake with quartered slices of lemon. Cut into slices and serve with a spoonful of crème fraîche.

Serves 8

> **TIP**
> ■
> Stir a little of the ginger syrup into the crème fraîche before serving or use fromage frais as an alternative.

STRAWBERRY
LAYER GATEAU

This is a classic summer dessert. Now that English strawberries are available from June to September, you can make it right through the summer months. You will need two 18-cm/7-in sandwich tins, which have been greased and floured.

175 g/6 oz soft vegetarian margarine
175 g/6 oz caster sugar
175 g/6 oz white self-raising flour
3 free-range eggs, beaten
$\frac{1}{2}$ teaspoon vanilla essence
2 teaspoons hot water
600 ml/1 pint whipping cream
150 ml/5 fl oz Kirsch or other liqueur
450 g/1 lb fresh strawberries
100 g/4 oz flaked almonds, toasted

■ Preheat the oven to 190°C/375°F/Gas Mark 5.
■ Put the margarine, caster sugar, self-raising flour, eggs, vanilla essence and hot water into a mixing bowl and beat until smooth. Divide equally between the two prepared cake tins and bake in the preheated oven for about 20 minutes, until the sponge is golden and springs back to the touch.
■ Leave to cool in the tins for 5 minutes, then turn out onto a wire rack and allow to cool completely. Cut each sponge in half horizontally so that you have 4 layers.
■ Whip the cream until stiff and fold in the Kirsch. Put about a quarter of the cream to one side for the decoration.
■ Reserve 6 evenly-sized strawberries and slice the rest. Spread each layer of sponge with some cream and top with the strawberries. Make sure you leave enough cream to coat the top and sides of the gâteau. Smooth the top.
■ Coat the sides of the gâteau with toasted almonds. Use the reserved cream to pipe rosettes on the top. Halve the reserved strawberries and use to decorate. Chill until required.

Serves 6–8

Opposite: Strawberry layer gâteau

LEMON
MILLE FEUILLES

Light and refreshing, this fresh-tasting citrus dessert is an excellent dairy-free end to a meal.

225 g/8 oz ready-made puff pastry
a little soya milk, for brushing

300 ml/½ pint water
50 g/2 oz vegan margarine

Lemon filling:
4 tablespoons cornflour
50 g/2 oz caster sugar
zest of 2 large lemons
juice of 1 lemon

To garnish:
150 ml/¼ pint soya cream
icing sugar for dusting
4 strawberries, fanned
4 sprigs of fresh mint

■ Preheat the oven to 200°C/400°F/Gas Mark 6.
■ Roll out the pastry and cut into 4 pieces, 7 x 12 cm/3 x 5 in. Place on a greased baking sheet, brush with soya milk and cook in the preheated oven for 10-15 minutes. When risen and golden, remove from the oven and allow to cool on a wire rack, then separate each piece into 3 layers.
■ Mix the cornflour and sugar together in a bowl. Add enough water from the measured 300 ml/½ pint to mix to a smooth paste.
■ Put the rest of the water and the lemon zest in a saucepan, bring to the boil and then pour over the cornflour and sugar mixture, stirring until smooth.
■ Return to the saucepan and bring back to the boil, stirring all the time. Reduce the heat and simmer for 1 minute. Remove from the heat, and beat in the margarine and then the lemon juice. Allow to cool and thicken.
■ Beat the lemon mixture thoroughly until smooth and shiny. Keeping the layers of pastry in the right order, spread half the lemon mixture on the bottom slices, top with the middle slices and spread the remaining mixture over these. Top with the final pastry layers and place on serving plates.
■ Pour a little soya cream around the plate. Dust each mille feuille with icing sugar and decorate with a fanned strawberry and mint sprigs.

Serves 4

TIP

■

Try to use the ready-made but not ready-rolled puff pastry for this recipe. It rises better and can be split into layers more easily. Even better, make your own! For a special occasion the flavour and rise of a home-made puff pastry is well worth the effort.

FLORENTINES

These contrast well with the pear and stem ginger sorbet on page 106. You can use any mixture of nuts and fruits that you fancy to change the flavour of these delicate biscuits. The chocolate coating is optional.

50 g/2 oz butter or vegan margarine*
50 g/2 oz caster sugar
25 g/1 oz blanched, chopped almonds
25 g/1 oz chopped roasted hazelnuts
50 g/2 oz vegetarian glacé cherries, chopped
25 g/1 oz mixed peel, finely chopped
2 teaspoons lemon juice
100 g/4 oz vegan plain chocolate*

■ Preheat the oven to 180°C/350°F/Gas Mark 4. Line 2 baking sheets with non-stick baking parchment.
■ Melt the butter or vegan margarine* in a saucepan. Add the sugar and boil the mixture for 1 minute, stirring all the time. Remove the pan from the heat and add all the remaining ingredients, except the chocolate, and stir well to mix.
■ Drop the mixture in very small heaps onto the prepared baking sheet, allowing each room to spread (9 on each sheet).
■ Bake in the preheated oven for 10–15 minutes, until golden brown (watch carefully as the edges tend to burn). Remove from the oven and use the edge of a knife to neaten the edges of the biscuits. Leave on the baking sheets to cool.
■ Melt the chocolate over a bowl of simmering water (or for 2–3 minutes in microwave). Take each biscuit off the baking parchment and spread chocolate thinly over the smooth (flat) side. Leave to start setting and just before it sets use a fork to mark wavy lines in the chocolate. Leave to cool completely.

Makes 18

TIP
■
Make sure you leave these little biscuits to cool completely before you try to remove them from the baking parchment as they are quite fragile.

CHOCOLATE AND
CHESTNUT TORTE

This is a very rich dessert, especially for chocoholics! You only need a small slice but will probably be tempted to have more!

50 g/2 oz plain chocolate
50 g/2 oz unsalted butter
2 free-range eggs, separated
50 g/2 oz sweetened chestnut
  purée
12 g/½ oz plain flour
good pinch of cream of tartar
1 tablespoon granulated sugar

Topping:
350 ml/12 fl oz double cream
4 tablespoons Tia Maria or other
  coffee liqueur
50 g/2 oz plain chocolate, grated
  very finely (use food processor disk)
chocolate coated coffee beans
  (optional)

■ Preheat the oven to 180°C/350°F/Gas Mark 4. Grease and then line a 20-cm/8-in loose-bottomed cake tin.

■ Break the chocolate into small pieces and place them with the butter in a bowl over a pan of gently simmering water. Stir until melted and smooth.

■ Put the egg yolks, chestnut purée and flour in a large bowl and whisk together. Stir in the melted chocolate and butter mixture.

■ Whisk the egg whites and cream of tartar together in a grease-free bowl until they form soft peaks. Then gradually sprinkle on the granulated sugar and whisk the mixture until stiff. Gently fold into the chocolate mixture, using a metal spoon.

■ Pour into the prepared cake tin and level the top. Cook in the preheated oven for 35–40 minutes. Allow to sit for 5 minutes, then remove the cake from the tin and leave to cool on a wire cooling rack.

■ To make the topping, whisk the double cream until stiff and gently fold in the Tia Maria.

■ Spread a layer of cream over the top of the torte and then, using a piping bag and star nozzle, pipe rosettes around the edge of the torte. Sprinkle the grated chocolate over the centre and, if liked, decorate the edge with chocolate coated coffee beans. Chill for at least 2 hours, or until required.

Serves 8–10

CHOCOLATE ESPRESSO
AND ROASTED PECAN TORTE

This cake is extremely rich and luxurious, but completely dairy-free. It is ideal for any celebration. The addition of espresso gives the flavour an exciting twist. This quantity makes a very large torte. You may prefer to bake it in two tins and sandwich together with some of the fudge icing.

TIP
∎

Serve with a mixture of colourful fresh fruit, such as strawberries, kiwi, melon and peaches, cut into chunks and threaded on skewers to make kebabs. Not only does this look exciting but the fruit helps to freshen the palette after the richness of the torte.

1.3 litres/2¼ pints boiling water
200 g/7 oz creamed coconut
2 tablespoons powdered espresso
 coffee
800 g/1 lb 12 oz self-raising flour
100 g/4 oz cocoa powder
2 teaspoons baking powder
100 g/4 oz roasted pecans
300 g/12 oz light muscovado
 sugar

420 ml/14 fl oz vegetable oil
2 tablespoons brandy

Fudge icing:
100 g/4 oz vegan margarine
2 teaspoons brandy
100 g/4 oz cocoa powder
6 tablespoons water
550 g/1 lb 4 oz icing sugar
few drops of vanilla essence

∎ Preheat the oven to 180°C/350°F/Gas Mark 4. Grease and line a 27.5-cm/11-in cake tin.
∎ Dissolve the espresso coffee in 2 tablespoons of the boiling water.
∎ Place the creamed coconut in a large bowl and cover with the remaining boiling water. Stir until dissolved.
∎ Mix together the flour, cocoa powder, baking powder, pecans and sugar.
∎ Add the espresso coffee to the cake mixture with the oil. Stir thoroughly, then add the cooled, dissolved coconut mixture and incorporate well.
∎ Pour the mixture into the prepared cake tin and bake in the preheated oven for approximately 1½ hours, or until the cake feels springy to the touch. Leave to cool slightly before turning out onto a cooling rack. When the cake is cool, drizzle with the brandy.
∎ To make the fudge icing, put all the ingredients in a food processor and blend until smooth. Spread the icing evenly over the cake and then use a fork to make an attractive pattern across the top.

Serves 12–16

INDEX

THE VEGETARIAN SOCIETY

The Vegetarian Society is the official voice of vegetarianism in the United Kingdom. The Society exists to promote Vegetarianism in the UK and throughout the world through research, national campaigns, education, liaison with the food industry and via our cookery school. A registered charity established in 1847, the Society is the leading authority on vegetarian issues, providing expert information on the vegetarian diet, for the benefit of animal welfare, human health and the environment. The Society provides information and resources for use by the public, media, health professionals, schools, and opinion formers.

Members of the Society receive a full-colour quarterly magazine full of the latest news, features and recipes, a discount card for use at hundreds of establishments, a unique seedling logo badge, access to our membership hotline and reduced rate subscription to *BBC Vegetarian Good Food* or *Wildlife* magazines. Membership support is vital to the Society's promotional and campaigning work. Members can become actively involved in the Society's work through the local group network or through the Council of Trustees, elected from the members.

The Society runs its own cookery school, Cordon Vert, the home of excellent vegetarian cuisine. The School runs inspirational courses to suit all abilities and interests from day courses through to a four-week Diploma course. Whatever your interest — Italian, Middle Eastern, Indian or Thai cuisine — the Cordon Vert has something to offer.

The Society works with major food manufacturers and retailers to improve the quality, quantity and variety of vegetarian food available. The Society also runs its own labelling scheme, known as the seedling symbol, approving over 2,000 products which are guaranteed to be 100 per cent vegetarian.

The Vegetarian Society needs membership support if it is to continue to operate at all levels to spread the vegetarian message. For a free vegetarian starter pack or details of the Cordon Vert Cookery School, please call us on 0161 928 0793 or write to the address below:

The Vegetarian Society
Parkdale
Dunham Road
Altrincham
Cheshire WA14 4QG

Internet address: www.vegsoc.org